Astrology

a psychological approach

COMPASS OF MIND

Knowledge is a dangerous thing, as Adam and Eve found out in the Garden of Eden. Yet without it, humanity would not evolve. Knowledge leads to new pathways of understanding, shaping our views of the world and extending our ability to create. Sometimes ways in which to apply knowledge are sought; at others, knowledge itself is enough, for it is said that man is made in the image of God, and, through knowing himself, can know the divine.

The series "Compass of Mind" is founded in this view of an integrated physical, human and spiritual universe. It looks at various ways in which knowledge is discovered and formulated, drawing themes from mystical and esoteric traditions, from the creative arts, and from therapies and broad-based science. For each topic the questions are posed: "What kind of a map of the world is this?" and "What special insights does it bring?" The series title embodies the concept that knowledge begins and ends with mind; a question asked expands into a circle which is both defined and investigated by mind itself.

Authors of "Compass of Mind" titles bring a wide perspective and a depth of personal experience to their chosen themes. Each text is written with clarity and sympathy, attractive to the lay reader and specialist alike. Themes are illustrated with lively, well-researched examples, aimed at revealing the essence of the subject, for these are books which tackle the question of "Why?" rather than "How to?"

Cherry Gilchrist, series editor

ASTROLOGY

a psychological approach

EVE JACKSON

DRYAD PRESS LIMITED
LONDON

To Molly

© Eve Jackson 1987
First published 1987
Typeset by
Progress Filmsetting Limited
79 Leonard Street, London EC2
Printed by Biddles Ltd
Guildford
Surrey
for the publishers
Dryad Press Limited,
8 Cavendish Square,
London W1M 0AJ

ISBN 0 8521 9699 7

CONTENTS

ACKNOWLEDGMENTS

I would like to thank Dave Stevens for his comments, suggestions and support during the writing of this book, and Cherry Gilchrist and Ruth Taylor for the pains they have taken in helping to produce a readable text.

The cover illustration is by Gila Zur.

Chapter 1

Symbols and Patterns

Most of us are conditioned by our education to view the world about us in rational, cause-and-effect terms. The irrational and the symbolic are allowed a place only in art, and perhaps in religion as something divorced from ordinary reality. Cultural conditioning over the last two or three centuries has tended to deny recognition of the symbolic level of reality, claiming for the scientific view a monopoly on truth. While many practical benefits have accrued to us from the application of the fact-based scientific method we believe to be so entirely rational, it is nonetheless the case that we can also be richly rewarded by an appreciation of the symbolic dimension to life, which runs in parallel to the factual dimension without in any way invalidating it.

The practice of astrology employs processes of very careful measurement, the precise calculation of the positions of sun, moon and planets along celestial co-ordinates, as seen from a point on the earth at a particular moment in time; in other words, it uses some of the tools of what is now the separate science of astronomy. For these measurements to yield meaning, however, a further, different process is involved. The *astronomer* seeks to comprehend the physical nature of the heavenly bodies and their motions, and the causes that determine these, by combining observation with theory. The *astrologer* is looking for a different kind of meaning, and this is communicated in the non-rational language of symbols.

When an astronomer speaks of the moon, he means a solid, spherical object orbiting the earth at a distance of nearly 239,000 miles. When an astrologer speaks of the moon she is using a symbol which reverberates with meaning; which evokes the lunar gods and particularly goddesses of earlier religions with their various attributes; which suggests the rhythm of waxing and waning, growth and decline, oceanic ebb and flow; which implies the mysterious night-time landscape, poetry and imagination. The precision of the calculations enables the astrologer to draw out the meanings of the astrological symbols in very specific contexts and in relation to specific times, but the symbols are capable of speaking on several levels at once so that they cannot, at least in natal or birth chart astrology which is the subject of this book, be translated with certainty into specific concrete events. Rather they evoke the probability of experiences of a particular nature. For example, a slowing down and grounding or a feeling of being obstructed is indicated by the symbolism of Saturn, bringing a sense of the limitations inherent in a particular circumstance and at the same time raising issues of material security, paternal authority and/or responsibility, and pointing to the suitability of dealing with the situation in a realistic and structured way. All of these associations come together in Saturn.

A symbol in this sense is not an item that can simply be translated into another term, like a road sign for motorists which is as far as possible unambiguous, and can be straightforwardly and completely interpreted into a word or two: One Way Street or Children Crossing. An astrological symbol is rich with connotations and is never entirely exhausted by the interpreter but always capable of producing new insights.

Such symbols speak not only to our intellect but also to an older, non-rational part of us, and are available to those who cannot read or write. We meet the symbolic realm in our dreams, where images gleaned mostly from our waking experiences recombine in ways that can appear crazy and irrelevant to the conscious mind but which, if we are attentive, can afford great insights into ourselves. Dream experiences of drowning or burning or flying may be conveying emotional states or inner processes that we are not fully conscious of; dream figures, human or animal, are aspects of our inner world. The very private and personal experience of dreams uses symbols which are also shared; we find them again in poetry and the arts and in our religious and cultural traditions.

Religion, which necessarily deals with that which cannot be conveyed fully in words, relies considerably on symbolic rituals and images. We may think, for example, of the Christian feast of the mass, and what it means to be symbolically partaking of the flesh and blood of God incarnate; or of the Buddhist symbolism of the lotus. The lotus has its roots in the mud; its stem grows up through the water; it produces leaf and bud on the surface, in the air; the flower opens up to the light and warmth of the sun. This symbol expresses something about a development from darkness to light, a connection between lower and upper. As the lotus grows, it makes use of the four elements, earth, water, air and fire, which we will encounter again in this book. The flower opens fully, its many layers of petals forming a circle, offering itself freely to all. Much more could be said about this image and its relationship to the spiritual path or the fulfilment of individual potential, but I hope it can be seen already that there is a great deal to explore in a symbol, and that it is not a simple equation.

What we call superstitions are often survivals from older religions, and date from a time when people were more in touch with the symbolism of everyday life. My mother used to get very anxious when she saw the new moon (which she normally looked forward to seeing) through glass, and she was not alone in this. I think that probably the original meaning of the expression "to see the new moon through glass" was rather different from our present understanding. In the Authorised Version of the Bible St Paul tells us that in our ordinary mortal condition we see "through a glass, darkly" (I Corinthians, xiii, 12), and this is retranslated in the Jerusalem Bible as "a dim reflection in a mirror". The Jacobean English has lingered on in the folk saying, and if we convert it into the modern expression, to see the new moon *in* a glass or mirror, the superstition makes much more sense. The young crescent moon (which curves to the right) conveys a sense of promise, of a fresh start, of growth to come, but if we see it reversed in a mirror then it takes on the form of the old, waning moon, soon to be darkened completely. It is obvious why symbolically this conversion of the new moon into the old should have a sinister feel to it, suggestive of hopes crushed or of things coming prematurely to an end. Appropriately, the moon itself, which reflects the light of the sun, is sometimes associated in astrology with mirrors.

Now I am not suggesting that we should all make a point of worrying more about walking under ladders and the rest, but I do wish to imply that if we are open to this kind of symbolism it is perfectly possible that we may intuit meanings in the images that strike us in waking life, just as we may by exploring the symbolism of our dreams. The recognition of such symbolic meanings can permit the transmission of messages from another level of consciousness.

Let me give an example of the kind of thing I am talking about. I hope you will forgive the fact that it is a rather sinister example that comes to mind. Some years ago I was in Nepal and arrived back at my lodgings one evening to find a black scorpion on my door. I had never actually seen a scorpion before, but the image struck immediate horror into me; I felt it like a blow in the solar plexus. I managed to unlock the door and shake off the creature so that it scuttled away, but the feelings of unease and ominousness which the encounter had aroused in me, even though I established that that particular type of scorpion was not of the most poisonous, could not so easily be shaken off. A few days later a telegram reached me to say that my father had had a stroke. From this he eventually died, although not before I had arrived home to see him. The astrological sign of Scorpio is of course associated with death, and perhaps this knowledge had contributed to my uneasy feelings. More recently a client, also a student of astrology, told me a similar story. While on holiday she picked up a sheet and found to her horror a scorpion on it. That night she was bothered by unpleasant dreams which she tried to banish from her mind. Then news arrived that her father had died. In both cases the scorpion was felt to herald fatal news and was meaningful to both of us through our knowledge of a particular symbolic language.

This kind of openness to symbolism is necessary in the practice of astrology, as it is in numerous other traditions such as the Kabbalah and the Tarot. It also reconnects us with that aspect of the psyche which communicates through pictures rather than concepts. In physiological terms this involves the functions usually performed by the right brain. (As a general rule our activities tend to be dominated by the left brain, the seat of logical operations and linguistic constructs). In this way astrology brings us closer to art than to science and complements that rational picture of the world which is less than the whole truth, but which in our culture we are inclined to overvalue.

A horoscope or astrological chart is a map showing the positions of the sun, moon and planets along the circular path of the zodiac (in Greek="the path of the animals") in relation to a particular time and place on earth. The zodiac is a circular strip of sky like a hat-band, straddling the apparent path of the Sun (the *ecliptic*). If one imagines the zodiac as a road, the ecliptic is the white line that defines the middle. Although there are other ways of drawing up such a map, the form most people are familiar with, at least in the

West, is that of a circle with geometrical divisions, containing the planets. (In astrology the sun and moon are included in the term "planets", which in Greek means simply "wanderers" or moving bodies.) The basic circle of the chart represents the circle of the zodiac in the sky, but the circular design with its component elements is also symbolic: like the lotus flower it is a kind of mandala.

A mandala (a Sanskrit word simply meaning "circle") is an object of contemplation. A circle encompassing a geometric pattern, it is an image both of the universe and of our own potential wholeness. It is a form of sacred art used to carry the mind of the meditator into the realisation of the unity of all things, and complex mandalas are visualised inwardly in some Hindu and Buddhist forms of practice. Equivalent figures, conveying a sense of order, wholeness and centrality, are found world-wide. God has been described as a circle whose centre is everywhere, whose circumference nowhere, and we can also imagine ourselves as being at the centre of our own mandala. Plato thought that the original human beings were spherical, subsequently split into hemispheres which became the male and female of the species, always seeking to be re-united in their original wholeness. In fact, when children first start to draw human figures they generally draw them as circular, with little arms and legs appended, even though this does not correspond to what they see with their eyes[1]*, and so this identification with the circle comes very naturally to us.

The circle has no beginning and no end, thus symbolising eternity; and by joining opposites it symbolises unity. Left and right, up and down meet in the circle; by travelling around the world to westwards we can arrive in the east. But the mandala typically combines the unity of the circle with geometrical figures made of straight lines which divide that unity into parts. Generally these involve squares or crosses, sometimes triangles. Our visible horizon is a circle

*For Notes, see page 154.

at whose centre we find ourselves, but in order to have some sense of direction we superimpose on it the four cardinal points, north, south, east and west, and from this we can get further subdivisions and greater accuracy — we can travel south-south-east, for example.

The mandala thus contains the idea of the One and the Many, the ultimate unity of all things in the circle and the innumerable manifestations into which it can be divided up, and the zodiac too represents both unity and multiplicity. It has its own four cardinal points, the beginnings of the signs Aries, Cancer, Libra and Capricorn, where the sun finds itself at the spring equinox, summer solstice, autumn equinox and winter solstice, respectively. Each quarter is then divided into three signs, and the signs also have various kinds of subdivisions. On every chart the entire complement of signs is there, the circle is complete, and the planets are each located in a sign. Seen from the earth, which is our central point of reference as earth-dwellers, the sun moves around the zodiac during the course of a year, passing through each sign for a month. "John is a Sagittarius" means that the sun was in the sign of Sagittarius at the time of John's birth, and the glyph for the sun, a circle with a dot in the middle, will be shown against the section representing that sign on his birth chart or horoscope. The sun sign (popularly known as the "star sign") is important, but it is also important to be aware that, as the circularity of the horoscope suggests, we each have all twelve signs on our chart, symbolising the idea that we each contain the full range of human possibilities, although we develop some at the expense of others. I may, for example, be pushed to develop the qualities of Leo because it is my sun sign, and of Pisces because it is my moon sign, but since I have no planets in Taurus the qualities of Taurus will have less relevance for me. Taurean vices will not be my problem, and Taurean virtues will not be my strong point.

At this point it is perhaps necessary to make clear that the signs of the zodiac we use in the West, those of the so-called "tropical" zodiac, do not coincide in the sky with the constellations after which they were originally named. The beginning of the *sign* of Aries, which is considered the first sign of the zodiac, is calculated from the sun's position at the spring equinox, but due to a wobble in the earth's spin this point is no longer in the *constellation* Aries, but is moving in the opposite direction to the motion of the planets, from the constellation Pisces into the constellation Aquarius. This is what we mean when we say that we are moving into the age of Aquarius. The equinoxial point slips gradually around the constellations, returning to the same point in about 25,000 years. This period with its twelve ages is known as a Great Year, one of the many cycles in which we are participating.

The number twelve has the virtue of being divisible in a number of different ways, so that the signs can be grouped into six pairs, four sets of three signs each, three of four, or two of six, leading to great complexity of meaning. Particularly important are the four elements (fire, earth, air and water), to each of which three signs belong, and the three qualities (cardinal, fixed and mutable), to each of which four signs belong.

In the ancient world, the Pythagoreans taught that the material universe was composed of four elements, and it was a natural inference that the microcosm of the human being was composed in the same way of solid matter, fluid, air and warmth. That is physical reality, but the elements are also a natural and ancient source of symbolism which lives in our dreams, stories and everyday speech. Air, and to some extent fire which moves upwards and illuminates us from the heavens in the form of the sun and stars, suggest height and the spirit which strives upwards, while earth and water are gravity-bound, and water in particular suggests depth and mystery. Fire and air are traditionally masculine, earth and water feminine.

Water renews, refreshes, cleanses, dissolves, takes on the form of any container without having its own shape; it reflects images. In baptism we return symbolically to the waters of the womb. We use the image of waves, sometimes tidal waves, of emotion, of still waters that run deep, of pools of tranquillity, of a sense of flow in our lives or the lack of it. Tidal flux is connected with the moon, astrologically a watery planet.

Earth is heavy but useful, clay to be moulded, stone and bricks for houses; Saint Peter was the rock or support on which the Church was to be built. Earth can mean hard, incontravertible facts, calling a spade a spade. Mother earth was seen as the provider of all good things, greenness, golden corn, fruits and flowers, and she is also the dust our bodies come from and return to.

Air is light and comes and goes with our breath and speech. It is boundless space and the element of winged creatures. It represents the possibility of rising above the earth and seeing things in perspective, with detachment, perhaps losing touch with the ground, or getting above ourselves like Ikaros who flew too high and had to fall.

Fire not only burns and consumes with volcanic passions, warms our hearts, fires our enthusiasm, and kindles our imagination, but also lights us up and brightens our darkness. It cleanses by destroying, and yet it can be the spark of creativity.

The sequence of elements in the zodiac (Fire-Earth-Air-Water) interlaces with the sequence of qualities. The cardinal signs come first and get things moving; they are followed by the fixed signs which consolidate and hold on; last come the mutable signs, loosening things up and free to move with the wind.

The geometry of the signs is pretty: if we connect up the four belonging to the same quality, let us say the four cardinal signs (Aries, Cancer, Libra and Capricorn), we get a square or cross, with each sign connected belonging to a

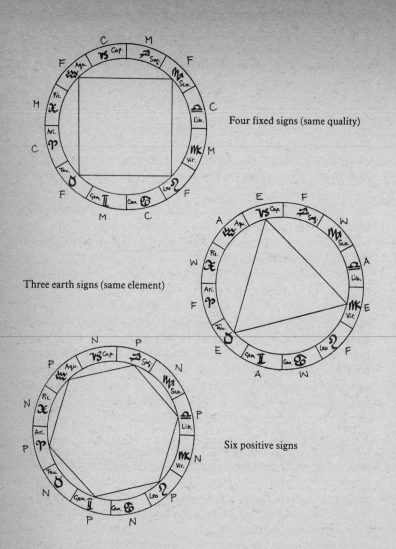

Four fixed signs (same quality)

Three earth signs (same element)

Six positive signs

Figure 1   Sign groupings

different element (Figure 1). If we connect the three signs belonging to one element, this forms a triangle consisting of one cardinal sign, one fixed and one mutable. The cross formed by the four elements gives a picture of completeness and complementarity, co-existence in space, while the three qualities suggest movement through time: beginning (cardinal signs), middle (fixed signs) and end (mutable signs), or go, stop, manoeuvre. Alternate signs are also given the value of masculine (fire and air) and feminine (earth and water), sometimes called positive and negative, comparable to the Chinese yang and yin. Connecting up one of these two groups of signs forms a hexagon. There is also a particular relationship between opposing signs, which are always both feminine or both masculine and share some kind of common theme. Those with opposite sun signs are often attracted to each other and tend to make good marriage partners.

This is all beautifully symmetrical and serene, but this mandala, common to all charts, can have any sign at the top, depending on the time of day for which the chart is drawn, and against this matrix the planets appear, peppered in an irregular and unique pattern. There is no such thing as a typical chart. Viewed from the earth, all the planets move round the zodiac in the same direction (Aries-Taurus-Gemini . . . Pisces), but at different speeds. The sun completes the circuit in a year, the moon in a month, Mars in two years, whilst the planets farthest from the sun move very slowly, and spend years in a single sign. Pluto, the outermost, takes nearly 250 years to move through the twelve-part cycle. Each of these bodies carries its own symbolism, and also takes on a coloration from the sign it is passing through. If we imagine each of the twelve signs and ten moving heavenly bodies as having a different colour, we can visualise what an enormous variety of shades and patterns there could be. The geometrical relationships between the planets and the patterns they form are also significant. Each chart is as individual as a thumb print.

Since the planets move through the signs, always in the

same direction, the zodiac can also be thought of as a sequence, starting with the fiery thrust of Aries and finishing with the dissolution of watery Pisces, out of which Aries springs anew. Also, the whole circle appears to be rotating about us, because of the earth's own rotation, each sign rising up over the eastern horizon in succession. The zodiac is thus not only a mandala but also a wheel, related to other wheel images such as the Wheel of Fortune in the Tarot, and suggestive of perpetual rising and falling. Fortuna was a very popular goddess in Rome, as the deity who might favour us by carrying us up rather than down.

Another wheel figure is the Tibetan Wheel of Life, a circular image from Buddhism. The stages of life from birth to death are depicted round the circle, in a way reminiscent of the progression from Aries to Pisces. But the wheel also contains pictures of six realms of existence, varying from blissful to horrific, through which beings are imagined to roll on from incarnation to incarnation, up and down, continuing on a bigger scale the vicissitudes of this life. The alternation of pleasant and unpleasant states of existence can, instead of being taken literally to refer to successive lives, be understood as an analogy for the ups and downs of our emotions within the present life.

The view of life as a cyclic process is fundamental to astrology, whether or not one extends it to reincarnation, as some astrologers do, for it is reflected in the perpetual circling of planets and of the sky itself, and in other cycles such as that of the Great Year. It is true that we never return to *exactly* the same situation, but so it is in the heavens: when one planet has come full circle, the others will all be in different places from before. As to whether astrology implies reincarnation, the latter is simply one way of answering one of the questions the birth chart poses, namely, what is the cause of a person being born with a particular chart? Perhaps, however, it is not necessary to think of astrology in terms of causality at all.

An astrological chart may be calculated for other purposes, but in this book our primary concern is the chart drawn up for the time and place of birth of an individual, and the mysterious way in which the pattern on the chart appears to reflect the pattern of the individual life: the characteristic tendencies, the typical recurring situations, and the tides and seasons of life — times to sow and to reap, high points, low points, turning points. With the horoscope in mind, developments do not appear to be arbitrary, but form part of the meaningful web of our story, each new direction we take growing out of what has been before and preparing the way for what follows. However we choose to explain the connection between chart and person, astrology affirms that we must each dance to our own particular tune, improvising the steps as we go.

As our lives progress we weave our own stories, and though these are highly personal they have at the same time something typical about them. Falling in love, giving birth, separation, achievement, distintegration, feelings of anger, sorrow, joy are part of the human condition, and themselves tend to be grouped in certain patterns, so that an experience of death, say, is followed by grief and perhaps eventual renewal. These recurring human dramas are the substance of myths. Think of Ikaros, for example, who flew too high, too near the sun, and came crashing down into the sea. Do we not know or hear of people who live out such a pattern? Or Elektra, whose love of her father is equalled only by her hatred of her mother.

Such symbolic stories cluster about the astrological planets and signs; indeed the planets are named after Greco-Roman deities whose stories are still relevant to us, and who may be considered as externalised images of inner processes. It is as if I, the individual corresponding to "my" birth chart, contain a number of different personalities, the warrior, for example, the seeker, artist, clown, each seeking expression through a different set of possible scenarios, each relating well or awkwardly to the other, according to my particular pattern. The myths, then, live both on the horoscope and in our lives.

The glyphs used to represent the planets also have their significance, each being composed of a combination of circle and cross, the circle deemed to represent the eternal realm of spirit, and the cross standing for matter in all its divisibility. The semi-circle may be given the separate meaning of "soul", depending on your model of psychic anatomy. Saturn, for example, which is an earthy planet, has in its glyph the cross of matter uppermost, while the glyphs for the sun and moon, also called the "lights" ("according to her lights"), have no cross at all.

If you are able to gaze at the stellar pattern in the sky on a warm, clear night, you can begin to pick out the constellations which gave their names to the signs of the zodiac,* the bull, the lion, the fishes. Yet you have to work quite hard to join the dots and really see those beasts up there. It is not especially obvious why a particular star group should be seen, say, as a human being carrying a water jar. It doesn't exactly hit you that that is what is up there. Perhaps this is because those who first perceived this animal circle were looking with the inner eye as much as the outer, intuiting a symbolic pattern, a circular sequence of images which resonated in their innermost being, and that expressed itself in these figures, the twins, or the goat with a fish's tail, such as one might encounter in dreams. Looking at the starry heavens they saw the patterns hidden in themselves, in all of us. This understanding is expressed in the adage, "as above, so below".

*The *signs* are not identical with the *constellations* — see p. 14.

Chapter 2

Time and Space

Most people realise that in order to draw up a birth chart the *time* of birth is required, but time is always relative to a particular *place*. An international flight arrival needs to be defined as, for instance, 5.00am New York time, or Eastern Standard Time, and an astrological chart also requires a location. A horoscope is a time/space map.

Time

In the last chapter we looked at the circle of the zodiac, which appears to revolve around the earth and forms a backdrop against which the planets also circle. Another familiar circle which also generally has twelve divisions and involves a rotational element is the face of a clock, with its twelve numerals and two or three hands. Just as a planet reaches Pisces, the last sign, only to begin again with Aries, so each hand of the clock moves from twelve on to one again. Clock time is necessarily cyclic; this is less immediately apparent with a digital clock where no circle is seen, but it is still the case: the figures 12.59.59 revolve to reveal 1.00.00.

Imagine a clock with ten hands, each moving at a different speed. Consider how many cycles of the slowest-moving hand it might take before all ten came back to occupy exactly the same respective positions as they were in at a given moment. In the case of the planets moving round the zodiac the issue is considerably complicated by the fact that, because the earth itself is moving relative to the other moving bodies, all planets (except the sun and moon) at times appear to be going backwards *(retrograde)* along the zodiac, that is to say from west to east. The question of how long it would take for a particular planetary pattern to repeat itself preoccupied ancient astronomer/astrologers, and they tried to calculate it; the Egyptians, for example, arrived at a figure of 30,000 years. When we remember that they knew of only seven planets (sun, moon, Mercury, Venus, Mars, Jupiter and Saturn) and that we have now discovered three more, the outermost of which (Pluto) takes nearly 250 years to complete its circuit, we have to start thinking in millions of years. And then perhaps we should make allowance for other bodies being found to complicate the issue further. Perhaps also we should consider the position of the equinoxial point, that is to say, regard the Great Year as another hand on the clock. To all intents and purposes we must conclude that our celestial clock is never going to tell the same time again, not during any period of time we can readily imagine, perhaps not even in the life of our solar system. Astrology, then, is dealing with unrepeatable moments.

Our primitive experience of time, before we encounter clocks, is also cyclic, or rhythmic. The baby has a cycle of sleeping and waking, of feeding and digestion, and even earlier it has experienced the rhythm of its own and its mother's heartbeat, its mother's own diurnal cycle of rest and activity, and so on. Night-time follows daytime, and then daytime comes round again, and after birth we soon register the rhythm of light and dark. When we are a little older we can observe the rhythm of the lunar changes and begin to get a sense of the period that separates one new moon from another. The geometrical simplicity of the circular full moon and the semi-circular moon at the first and third quarters makes the four-beat rhythm of the four-week lunar month an easily recognisable pattern. Eventually we familiarise ourselves with the repeating seasons and learn to think in years, with our birthday coming round at regular intervals. (The astrological equivalent to the birthday is the *solar return*, the moment when the sun reaches the exact point—degree and minute—where it was at our birth, and this does not always fall on the day we celebrate, but often on the day before or after our birthday.)

For pre-modern agricultural societies the rhythms of sun and moon were vital guides for planting, but animals who may lack our capacity to detach ourselves from nature and calculate consciously are also attuned to these cycles, as we can see from annual patterns of hibernation, migration, and fertility and the lunar cycles of some creatures. Plants also respond to lunar cycles as well as to the annual cycle marked by the position of the sun, and planting according to the lunar phase for the best results is a valuable part of agricultural lore. A number of unconscious physiological cycles have also been identified in the human body, some approximating to a day, some to longer periods, and some psychological conditions show cyclic patterns too.

Calendars developed long before clocks and were based on the cycles of moon phases and seasons. Their creation involved observation of celestial phenomena. What we normally refer to as the lunar cycle is in fact a sun/moon cycle, the new moon falling at the time when the sun and moon are in the same degree of the zodiac (in astrological terminology, *in conjunction*), so that the moon is between the earth and sun and presents its shadow side to us: it is then invisible from the earth. (In common speech we use the expression "new moon" to describe the slim, waxing crescent, but technically the term refers to the time when not even a sliver of shining moon can be seen. It is usually two or three days later that we spot it in the sky.) When the moon is full it is on the opposite side of the earth from the sun *(in opposition),* so that we are looking straight at the bright side of the moon which faces the sun. At the exact full moon sun and moon are 180 degrees apart on the zodiac, in opposite signs such as Aries and Libra. Recognising the lunar phases not only enabled people to sow seeds at the appropriate time but also made other kinds of planning possible. Two people could arrange to meet at a certain place at the next full moon, or a journey could be described and anticipated as taking so many moons. Apart from these practical uses the lunar cycle was awe-inspiring and symbolic, echoing the mysteries of the emergence of life, maturity, decline and death, so that the lunar phases, and in particular the new and full moons, were occasions of religious significance. The sabbath or day of rest probably developed from a holy day at the new moon, when the moon was deemed to be at rest or in the inward-looking phase of menstruation. It is easy to understand why the moon has most often been understood as corresponding to a feminine deity.

The moon, however, is not particularly helpful if we want to think in terms of seasons, which are based on the orbit of the earth round the sun. This is not signalled in such an obligingly obvious manner as the cycle from one new moon to the next but requires more persistent observation and recording. To ordain the days for those annual religious festivals which marked and still mark the passage from one season, or one year, to the next required considerable sophistication of calculations. Because of the tilt of the earth's axis relative to the path of its orbit, during one half of its cycle the northern hemisphere is inclined more towards the sun, and during the other half the southern hemisphere enjoys that privilege, with the north getting the maximum amount of daylight around 21st June and the south around 21st December. At the points half-way between these two dates the day and night are of the same length all over the world (the *equinoxes*, in March and

September), and from these points, as the days lengthen or shorten, the sun each day reaches a slightly higher or slightly lower point in the sky. When it reaches its highest point of the year (around 21st June in the northern hemisphere) its ascent ceases, and it begins to decline again, while in the southern hemisphere it stops declining and begins to climb again. These points are known as the *solstices*, meaning the times when the sun stands still.

It has taken millenia to arrive at our present-day calendar, valid for hundreds and thousands of years without slipping gradually out of phase with the actual round of seasons as was the case with earlier versions. Yet over three and a half thousand years ago Stonehenge seems to have served a calendar function, and still the sun at the summer solstice can be seen to rise along the main axis of the principal stone circle. It also appears that longer cycles than the annual earth/sun cycle, in particular the eclipse cycle of approximately nineteen years, could be predicted by means of this, one of the best-known of megalithic monuments. In this way, Stonehenge and other stone circles bear witness to an ancient recognition of the cyclic nature of time[2].

Our sixty-minute standard hour is a relatively recent invention — or re-invention, since thousands of years ago the Sumerians of Mesopotamia invented the sexagesimal system on which it is based and a division of the day into twenty-four hours. The clock hour reflects our movement away from the experience of observable natural cycles, with their various irregularities, towards standardised, uniform time units. Before the invention of the mechanical clock in about the fourteenth century, the most common type of clock was one that measured the length and/or angle of shadows thrown by the sun, such as a sun-dial, and this could obviously only be used to measure daylight hours, and only on sunny days. The day, varying in length according to the time of year, though to a lesser degree in the tropics, could then be subdivided from sunrise to sunset, and the length of the "hours" thus formed would vary. In some ancient systems each hour was ruled by a planet.

Another measurer of time that preceded the mechanical clock was the water clock or clepsydra, which allowed water to drip through a hole in a pot at a regular rate. The depth of the water remaining in the pot was measured, in the same way as the sand remaining in a sand glass. But, as far as is known, no attempt was made to produce a standard measure of time for dividing up day and night by means of such clocks until the imposition of a regular daily routine demanded it. It seems likely that this demand first came from the practice of organised religion. The first mechanical, weight-driven clock dated for certain was built in 1335 in the palace chapel of the Visconti. The development of the monastic orders in preceding centuries had involved the establishment of a sequence of services spaced throughout the day, and during the twelfth and thirteenth centuries a time-keeping monk had kept watch on an hour-glass or water clock and rung a bell to alert the brethren to the hour[3].

The mechanical clock developed to meet the requirements of collective routine, and created a new source of anxiety. Previously time had been measured as approximate periods between sunrise and noon, noon and sunset, with individuals simply making the most of the daylight hours and generally orientated towards the rhythms of nature, experienced in the environment and in the human body as the need for food and rest. Gradually, and particularly in cities, time came to be counted in a very precise fashion so that work and leisure periods could be objectively compared. The twenty-four hour day was established, starting when the sun was calculated to be at its lowest point below the horizon (midnight) and divided into hours of equal length, day and night, summer and winter. This meant the creation of *mean time*, which ironed out the slight variations in day length caused by irregularities in the earth's motion.

Mean time in this sense is *local mean time*, each clock being synchronised to show twelve o'clock roughly at the local midnight and midday points. However, for each fifteen degrees we travel east or west along the 360 degree circle of the earth's equator, or parallel to it, there is an hour's difference in local mean time. For example, the sun rises and sets at Truro in Cornwall approximately twenty minutes later than in London because it is about five degrees to the west of London. The development of the railways in the nineteenth century, enabling long-distance travel in a relatively short space of time, necessitated timetables and the invention of *standard mean time* so that all clocks within a country or section of a country could be synchronised. This means that instead of there being a gradual, imperceptible slipping forwards or backwards in relative time of day as we travel to west or east, we now travel for a considerable distance using one standard clock time and move at a given point into a zone with a time one hour or half-an-hour ahead or behind. The history of time measurement has thus seen us lose touch with the natural, visible timespans observed by the builders of Stonehenge and become increasingly conscious of, even obsessed with, a time of our own devising. It is thanks to this man-made time that we are able to erect horoscopes today with a greater degree of accuracy, but in the process of calculating an astrological chart we have to work back from the time shown on the clock face in standard mean time to divisions of the natural celestial cycles from which our clock time derives.

Cycles are also found in our individual life stories. The same experience comes round again, although the whole situation will not be exactly the same. It is not that I find myself in the same room again with the same individual, saying the same thing in the same words, but that some important factor is the same and I think, "Ah, I've been here before". It is as if one of the hands of our complicated clock-has returned to the same point. Astrologically this might mean, for instance, that Jupiter has returned to the conjunction with Venus on my chart, or the progressed moon has returned to the fourth house. In any case, faced with a very similar situation to one I have been through before, there is the possibility that this time I will handle it differently because I have learnt from the experience of the previous time, and because the intervening period of time has changed me.

This brings us to another aspect of time. While our experience of it on one level is cyclic, and all our ways of measuring it are based ultimately on cycles, we also have a sense of time as carrying us along in a straight line, as on a conveyor belt moving always in the same direction. Experience is not reversible; what has been done cannot be undone and the dead do not return. If I burn my cake I can replace it by making another so that my guests never know about my mistake, but I can never unburn the burnt cake. It has been written, as it were, on the akashic records, which according to an esoteric tradition are supposed to preserve all occurrences for all time like a universal memory. Whether the akashic records preserve in perpetuity every wisp of cloud or only the experiences of the conscious mind is a matter for metaphysical debate, but once that wisp has dispersed it will never again form the same cloud.

The vision of the inexorable march of linear time is deeply embedded in our Judaeo-Christian tradition, which outlines a course of history beginning with God's singular act of creation and ending, in the Christian version, with the Last Judgement. We are prisoners in time, and before and after time is eternity. A more optimistic modern version of this linear notion of time is the belief in continuous progress from a primitive past towards an ever-brighter and more enlightened future. This optimism, a feature of nineteenth-century evolutionary thought, is of course wearing a little thin, and many people now feel again that Armageddon is just around the corner. An opposite theory, current in antiquity and revived in the Renaissance, held that history was a progressive falling away from the Golden Age, located in the distant past like a happy childhood seen from the point of view of adult disillusion, with only deterioration to look forward to. One day, the story went, the Golden Age would come again. The Hindu view of time incorporates the linear idea of beginning, development and end of the world within the framework of cycles, a view contained in the image of days and nights of the creator Brahma, who sleeps after the world has come to an end and eventually reawakens to create it anew, so that the whole development from creation to destruction is infinitely repeated.

The image of linear time stretching from creation to the final judgement can be seen as an analogy of our own individual lives which invariably start with birth and end with death, each passing moment falling away into the past. The Mithraic god Aion (=eon) has a lion's head, devouring all like greedy time. As we get older we become more aware both of this inexorable progress forwards and also of the cyclic tendency of things to come round again. The interaction of these two aspects of time can be visualised as a helix, that is to say, in the form of the thread of a screw or of a spiral staircase — or perhaps a combination of many helices with different diameters.

Time is also sometimes thought of as a fourth dimension. The question arises, if we are moving along the time dimension in the one direction possible to us, do the past and future exist somehow simultaneously, like earlier and later reels of the movie we are starring in? And if this is so, is it possible to see what lies ahead or a long way behind? The fact is that some people seem able to predict future events, and they may or may not use astrology in the process. Here we run into the question of whether everything that happens is in fact predestined, a question which is taken up in Chapter 8. There is no infallible system for predicting events, however, in my experience, so that perhaps it makes more sense to think in terms of a number of possible futures running in parallel, with each choice we make eliminating some of those future possibilities, and perhaps opening up new ones further down the line. Or perhaps we could say that the future exists but is constantly being modified by the present. Such speculations leave us with no certainty that we are close to unravelling the mysteries of time. We live within it and cannot step outside to observe it.

There is one meaning of the word time for which the Greeks had a separate word and which is really what astrology is all about. The word *kairos* denoted the *right* time, the appropriate time or season for a particular development. It is a common occurrence in the history of science that the same discovery or invention is made at around the same time by individuals in different countries and working completely independently. On the other hand, there are individuals who meet with nothing but misunderstanding during their lifetime but become guiding lights for future generations; they are ahead of their time. Looked at astrologically, it can generally be seen why something happened at a particular moment, and why no amount of striving can force something into being when the time is wrong. The rightness of the moment has to do both with our own readiness and with the state of the world about us, and both are contained in the astrology of the moment.

In astrological symbolism time is principally associated with the figure of Saturn, the old man of the astrological pantheon. Saturn's name in Greek is Kronos, a name very close in sound to that of Chronos, the god of time. It is possible that the two words are ultimately related, although classical scholars generally discard this possibility. In any case, in the course of time the gods became conflated, seeming to have more in common than the similarity of name, so that the typical figure of Saturn or Kronos is that of Father Time with his sickle or scythe, who is also the Grim Reaper, Death, who stands at the limit of our personal span of time.

The sickle or reaping-hook of Saturn (the scythe is a relatively modern version, invented only in the fourteenth century of our era) brings together a number of ideas. In the myth, Kronos uses this implement to castrate his father Uranus before usurping his throne and seizing the role of chief divine progenitor, showing that these figures belong to the era when the masculine role in procreation was recognised — earlier myths of the Goddess do not always acknowledge this. Saturn is thus linked to the concept of fatherhood, and the planet, together with his sign Capricorn, is connected with the father, despite the fact that he is associated with the feminine element earth. Notice too that the figure of the reaper is also referred to as *Father* Time, and is often depicted carrying an hour-glass in his hand. Another traditional association of Saturn is with measurement in general, and time as we normally use the word is defined in terms of measurement, via calendar or clock: years, months, hours, minutes, seconds, time ticking away and bringing us nearer to our encounter with the reaper.

Apart from being the instrument to which he owed his power, Kronos' sickle was first and foremost an agricultural implement, used for harvesting crops in the fulness of time; Kronos/Saturn was an agricultural deity. The implications of the Grim Reaper as a death image are that death comes both as the fulfilment of life, the point at which our degree of fruitfulness is measured, and as a mowing down or cutting short. Of the Fates of antiquity, three female figures, one (Clotho) spun the thread of each individual life, the second (Lachesis) measured it and the third, Atropos who cannot be averted, cut it as the reaper cuts the grass. This is the moment of judgement, the end of time as far as the individual is concerned, the boundary beyond which we cannot go in life. Saturn is not the only astrological symbol connected with death, but he is fundamentally associated with all boundaries and limitations, particularly the limitation of being in the mortal, physical body.

So the sickle is the reaper's tool as well as being the emblem of Kronos' patriarchal power. It is also of course an image of the crescent or sickle moon we find on Islamic flags and works of art, and the glyph used to represent the moon in astrology, and the moon itself is a reminder of the cyclic processes at work in nature. Saturn the measurer rules the sign of Capricorn, the sign of the father, while the moon rules the opposite sign, Cancer, the sign of the mother. These two signs on the same axis bring together the notions of natural, rhythmic time and time as a system of measurement, of cyclic time and time that runs in a straight line and finishes at a certain point.

As mistress of cycles, the moon relates to the womb we come from and symbolically return to at death, as well as to the rhythmic fluctuations of life. She has to do with memories of the subjective past, the place we have come from, and her sign, Cancer, has a reputation for indulging in nostalgia. As she is the fastest-moving body, she is the principal indicator of time in horary astrology, that branch of the art whose function is to answer specific questions.

Saturn is also specifically associated in astrology with the past, that which has been given a definite form and has the authority of tradition. In this respect he is contrasted with Jupiter, another planet named after a patriarchal god but associated with prophecy, knowledge of the future. Whereas the person with a strong Saturn is inclined to hark back to tradition and proven methods, one who has a strong Jupiter has an eye to the future. The future as perceived by Jupiter is not usually something already written, though he may relate to intuitions of what is to come, but a realm of infinite possibilities, and on the whole of opportunities for improvement. The two planets together were traditionally known as the two great *Chronocrators,* or lords of time, because as the two slowest-moving planets known to our forebears they enabled measurement of relatively long spans of time. The time when Saturn returns to his original position on the birth chart, around the age of twenty-nine, is a highly significant moment, and the near twelve-year cycle of Jupiter is the basis of the Chinese twelve-year astrological cycle. The conjunction of the two planets recurs every twenty years, and a series of successive conjunctions falls in the fire signs, followed by a series in the earth signs, and so forth, so that we have not only the cycles of the individual planets as measures, but also the sub-cycles formed from the relationship between the two planets as they move from one conjunction to the next. In 1980-81 Jupiter and Saturn conjoined in Libra, an air sign, after 200 years of successive conjunctions in the three earth signs. One of the traditional associations of Saturn/Jupiter conjunctions is the death (Saturn) of the king (Jupiter), and it has been remarked that US presidents elected during the year of such a conjunction have all died in office, notably J. F. Kennedy in recent years. Reagan was also elected in such a year; he is still in office at the time of writing, but has experienced an assassination attempt. To the *Great Conjunctions* of Jupiter and Saturn have now been added those involving Uranus, Neptune and Pluto as historical markers.

In astrology it is the circling planets that measure passing time. After the moment frozen on the birth chart their courses in the sky continue, and their later positions can be related to the original (*natal*) positions through *progressions* and *transits*. These relationships between natal and progressed or transiting positions are then interpreted to describe developments at the corresponding time of life.

Space

Time is obviously of the essence of astrology, but time as
something measurable is a product of movement through
space. It is five o'clock only in relation to a particular place
on earth, otherwise what the clock says is as arbitrary as the
time on the Mad Hatter's watch, and as Einstein has shown,
a clock speeding through interstellar space would speed up
relative to a clock on the earth. Since Einstein's revolution
we have acquired a concept of the relativity of space and
time, something fundamentally different from the New-
tonian vision of time as absolute and universal, ticking on at
a uniform rate everywhere.

Just as time brings us inevitably to the contemplation of
circular motions, so does space require us to think in
circles. Even before we knew that the earth was a sphere,
our perception of the horizon was of a circle with ourselves
at the centre, observable under ideal conditions (at sea, for
example, or from the top of a high tower) as a continuous,
unbroken line to the observer turning 360 degrees. The cross
or square of the four compass directions superimposed on
that circle to orientate us is a product of the human mind.
There are no straight lines in nature: even a Roman road
curves with the curvature of the earth's surface, and the
apparently straight line of an aircraft's vapour trail develops
into an arc. If we were to ascend vertically into the sky we
would again eventually find ourselves on a curving path
relative to the earth, because of the earth's continuing
rotation and orbit round the sun. According to Einstein,
space itself is curved.

The Ptolemaic model of the universe, which was
commonly accepted before Copernicus developed his
daring theory that the earth goes round the sun, also depicts
space by means of circles. The earth at the centre is
contained within a series of spheres corresponding to the
planets, with the circle of the zodiac lying beyond the
sphere of Saturn. The spheres beyond the moon were

held to be unchanging, with only the wretched sublunary realm in which we live out our earthly lives being subject to change and decay. According to this model, the soul rising up from the earth at death might be envisaged as travelling through these hierarchical spheres of increasing refinement and perfection.

We orientate ourselves in space by superimposing pairs of polar opposites upon it: up and down, left and right, before and behind, inner and outer, and all these co-ordinates have metaphorical meanings and values, though these are not absolute but vary according to the particular tradition. "Up", for example, is often considered to signify superiority (*superior* literally means "above"), above is the place of "higher orders" or greater proximity to God in Heaven while below falls to the Devil. We are generally describing a pleasant experience when we talk of feeling "high", and do not normally want to feel "down" or "low". On the other hand, we recognise that precious things are often found deeply buried. "Left" in Latin is *sinister*, and is also symbolically the feminine side. Western tradition tends to place greater value on the "outer world", but to the mystic the true world may be experienced as lying "within", in other words, closer to the centre.

The horizon is one of the circles fundamental to astrological calculations, and it is represented on the two-dimensional horoscope by a line running roughly from left to right, corresponding to east and west (the reverse of our usual geographical mapping procedure). Figure 2 illustrates this and other points raised in this paragraph. The second principal circle used is the equator; this is not shown on the chart, but as we have seen, measurement along the equator or one of its parallels is the means by which we arrive at the time in a given place. Both these circles are projected out into infinite space to become the *rational horizon* and the *celestial equator*. The third circle has already been described; it is the circle that frames the chart itself,

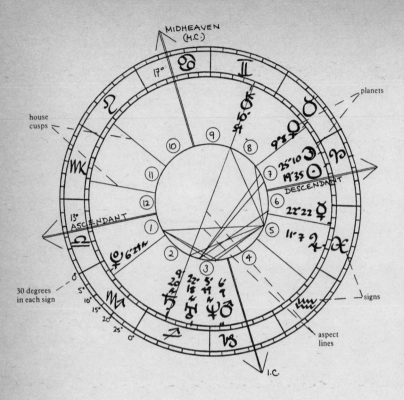

Figure 2   An astrological chart or horoscope

the circle of the ecliptic, along which are measured the signs of the zodiac (see page 11 for a more detailed description). It crosses the horizon at the ascendant to the east and the descendant to the west, rotating throughout the day in an anti-clockwise direction and carrying with it the planets, which are also moving anti-clockwise through the zodiac at their various speeds. At the top and bottom of the chart the ecliptic crosses a fourth circle, that of the north/south meridian, which passes through the north and south points of the horizon and the points above and below the observer

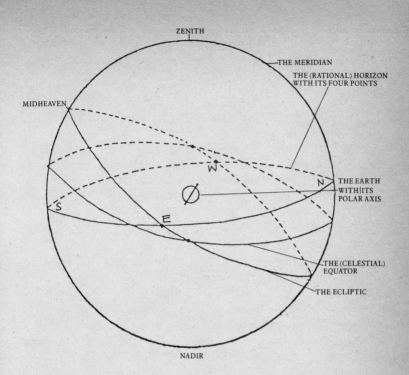

Figure 3   The celestial sphere (as set for an observer at the approximate latitude of London)

(the *zenith* and *nadir*). It crosses the upper meridian (due south on a northern hemisphere chart) at the midheaven (MC or *medium coeli*) and the lower meridian at the IC (*imum coeli*). The *ascendant, midheaven, descendant* and *IC* are the four all-important *angles* of the chart, the cross in the circle by which we orientate ourselves, and which forms the basis for a further subdivision into twelve houses. We can tell roughly what time of day an astrological chart is drawn up for from the position of the sun, which will be on the ascendant (left) at sunrise, midheaven (top) at noon, descendant (right) at sunset and IC (bottom) at midnight. Without an exact time a chart can have no orientation, no houses. These space circles are also shown in the celestial sphere diagram (Figure 3). Many museums have a three-dimensional celestial globe, and the relationships can scarcely be fully grasped without seeing one. Such a globe is a model of the heavens turned inside-out.

Astrologically it is the twelve houses that relate most specifically to space. The houses are formed from those four points in space known as the angles, and correspond to different "departments" of life, different rooms in the house of our experience, different locations of activity. They have been aptly compared to stage or film sets[4]: at the party, on the ship, in the bank, in the nursery, and so forth. The planets would then be the actors, or rather the types of roles they play such as the warrior/lover (Mars) who comes in and stirs things up, or the optimist (Jupiter) who raises hopes, gets you thinking, tempts you to overstep yourself and doesn't always come up with the goods. The circling signs of the zodiac, superimposed on the wheel of the houses, help write the script and develop characterisation, costume, scenery and style of production.

The individual chart is a unique meshing of all these time/space wheels. Birth into the world of time and space inevitably involves imperfection and decay, and the necessary imbalance of any particular chart, with its emphasis on certain signs, houses and planets, describes both our uniqueness and our limitations. The possibility of some other, unflawed kind of existence where the harsh rules of "this world" are suspended and there is no death, has been conceived in many forms, and described in terms both of time (the Golden Age, before the Fall, after the Last Judgement) and of space (Eden, Heaven, the Isles of the Blessed, the Western Paradise of Pure Land Buddhism). Terms relating to time and space are here used metaphorically; what is being described is a state of being. Such a state of timelessness and imperturbability is symbolised by the implied but invisible centre of the chart which neither rises nor falls, nor occupies any space. When we contemplate our own chart and become aware of the, inevitably, sometimes conflicting energies represented by the planetary configurations, we are staring at a reminder that the way to free ourselves is not by trying to become something different and wishing away our particular characteristics but by making contact with the still centre about which all the rest revolves. Viewed from that point, the antics of the planets in their signs and houses is mere play of patterns. In this mysterious image of ourselves that the birth chart presents is a zodiacal wandering about a timeless, spaceless centre.

Chapter 3

Science, Magic or What?

In astrology the symbolic attitude and ability to interpret signs combine with the awareness and measurement of cyclic time. What is the nature of the process which enables the astrologer to make judgements concerning people and events by combining measurement and interpretation? How does astrology work? I had better be frank from the outset and declare that I have no definitive answer to this question and can only attempt to outline some of the theories that have been proposed, or which are implicit in various forms of astrological practice.

Astrology is not a single system revealed at a particular point in time and practised henceforth without change, but has developed piecemeal over a long period. During this time (probably four thousand years, perhaps longer) there have been considerable changes in civilisation and consciousness, and these changes are reflected in the history of astrology and the way in which it has been understood at different stages by its practitioners. To understand how astrology came into being we have to look at its origins in Mesopotamia, the land between the Tigris and Euphrates (present-day Iraq), an area with a long cultural history under successive civilisations going back long before the establishment of the Hellenic tradition in Greece.

In Mesopotamia astrology grew out of the practice of omen-reading, which appears to be common to all cultures at a certain level of development. Reading omens or signs does not require a causal frame of reference; in fact it is possible to interpret signs without having any distinct notion of causality at all. While assertions about the history of consciousness, both of the species and within the developing individual, must remain largely speculative[5], numerous experiments on learning, using both humans and other species—even birds and fish—have demonstrated how fundamental to the learning process is the expectation that one event will follow another, based on past experience, regardless of whether or not causality is involved. In Pavlov's famous experiment, dogs salivated when a bell was rung, the ringing having previously been associated with a forthcoming meal.

If a dog caught and killed some prey, we could say that this hunting success was a cause of its having a meal, but we know that the bell was not a cause of the meal in the experiment: it was simply a *sign* that food was coming. We have no way of knowing for certain whether dogs and other non-human species are aware of this distinction, or whether it is one that developed at a certain point in human consciousness.

Causality is a complex issue. One event can have many causes (Aristotle distinguished between a number of different kinds of cause). In the case of the hunting dog, for example, the dog's hunger, its fitness, speed and skill, the co-operation of other members of the pack, the presence and lack of speed of the prey, the absence of other predators, the nature of the terrain and weather conditions might all be contributary causes of the dog's eating.

Experimenters in developmental psychology speak of a gradual acquisition of causal understanding in children. It could be argued, in fact, that causality is a social construction, a convention we have adopted for describing particular relationships between events.

A clear distinction between causal and non-causal relationships is certainly not necessary for reading something as a sign. (A *sign*, incidentally, does not have to be a symbol; Pavlov's bell did not *symbolise* food, it merely *signalled* it.) An associative process may be involved, which goes something like this: This morning on my way to my driving test my shoe-lace came undone. Last time I went to take the driving test my shoe-lace also came undone, and I failed the test. Perhaps this means that I am going to fail again. I know there can be no causal connection but I cannot help seeing this as a sign.

That the causal approach to events is not universally regarded as the obvious one is illustrated by Marie-Louise von Franz in *On Divination and Synchronicity*[6], a slim but concentrated book in which she devotes much space to the Chinese mentality. She claims that the Chinese tend to think in terms of clusters of events, asking themselves not "what will the effect of this event be?" but rather "what other events are likely to occur in association with it?" There are languages which contain no expressions for causal relationships, no "why?" or "because", such as that of the Trobriand Islanders, as reported by Canadian Professor Robert Bramwell in his *Semantics and Education*. This suggests that if the population in question has a sense of causality at all it cannot be more than rudimentary.

The omen-reading out of which astrology developed was, I am inclined to believe, based originally on a "cluster" approach rather than on a strictly causal one. In any case there appears to have been a long period when omens from the skies were read in a way that was not different in essence from, say, making predictions from the shape of smoke or from the patterns formed by tea leaves. The observation of sun, moon and planets moving against the background of fixed stars was not separate from the observation of other phenomena of the sky, such as the flight of birds and weather patterns: all of these signs provided a composite basis for prediction.

In a natural learning process such signs gradually came to be codified, probably first in an oral and later in a written tradition; intuitive perceptions were backed up by empirical data and handed on from one generation to the next. Over the centuries successive civilisations in Mesopotamia (Sumerians, Assyrians, Babylonians) kept detailed records of phenomena and predictions based on them.

Such a process of associating signs with forthcoming events is likely to have existed in very ancient pantheistic or animistic times, when divinity was not seen as something separate from nature but as dwelling in all natural phenomena. It probably existed when and where the only deity worshipped was the Goddess, who was manifest in all things and states, Mother Nature, lady of the eternal round of life, blindly giving birth and taking her children back again[7]. To the extent that anything had a cause, that cause was she. Whether or not some ultimate cause was deemed to lie behind signs, those in the heavens or elsewhere, it seems unlikely that the signs themselves were originally seen as causes.

Eventually, however, during the polytheistic era, the planets came to be identified with individual deities, thus distinguishing them from other interpretable phenomena. The names of the planets in fact changed with the pantheons of successive cultures in Mesopotamia. The predictive literature of the times, preserved on clay tablets, describes planetary movements in terms of activities of the gods, and offers prognostications concerning the affairs of king and kingdom. The deities themselves were seen as governing different aspects of existence, interacting with each other and influencing human life. In other words, the gods between them *caused* the range of experiences that befell mankind, and they could be observed in the sky. The will of the gods could be determined through other forms of divination, too, but only in the heavens, as planets, were the gods directly visible.

There is no reason to suppose that the fate of individuals other than the king or emperor, who embodied the welfare of the community as a whole, was a consideration. Divination, the process by which the will of the gods was determined, was the duty of a certain class of priests who recorded and collected the phenomena and their interpretations and communicated their findings to the king. Undoubtedly there was a more popular level of sign-reading, but literacy was the prerogative of the few, and there is no evidence that the body of divinatory data and theory accumulated by the priests was placed at the disposal of ordinary citizens.

From the time of the Sumerians, who created the first great civilisation of the land of Mesopotamia during the third millenium BC, the educated elite of that rich centre of culture were highly numerate as well as literate. They developed the sexagesimal system of counting which produced the hour composed of sixty minutes, each in turn composed of sixty seconds. Likewise they developed circular geometry, dividing the circle into 360 degrees, with sixty minutes to the degree and sixty seconds to the minute. Over the centuries, too, the movements of the planets came to be recorded, until it was realised that, as was the case with the sun and moon, the planets moved in a relatively fixed or stable circling fashion against the stellar backdrop.

There must have been a gradual development of awareness, so that instead of consulting the sky at a particular moment and making predictions on the basis of what was seen, it was possible to look ahead and imagine the positions of the planets at some time in the future, to foresee, let us say, that there would be a conjunction of Jupiter and Saturn the following year and interpret it accordingly. A very long period of accumulating observations, passed on at first by word of mouth, must have preceded the eventual compilation of tables of planetary movements (*ephemerides*), just as centuries of observation necessarily preceded the construction of Stonehenge if its function was indeed to predict celestial movements. The oldest ephemeris extant today dates from the end of the fourth century BC. By this time there had been considerable changes in Mesopotamian culture, following the end of independent rule in the region. First the area was bloodlessly taken over by the Persians in 538 BC. With the end of the empires of Assyria and Babylonia the power of the priests disintegrated and, no longer in the service of king and temple, they began to make their learning available to other interested parties. Astrology began to escape the tight hold of a strict religious tradition.

In fact, the sixth century BC saw a new spirit of enquiry and a secularisation of knowledge in other cultures, too. In Greece a number of philosophers of great stature (such as Thales, Pythagoras and Heraclitus) produced daring new theories on the nature of the universe, as the power and worship of the old gods faded; and in India Gautama Buddha challenged the Brahmin priesthood and exhorted his followers to seek with diligence their own paths to enlightenment, in a new atheistic mode. There is a kind of parallel with the secularisation of knowledge following the declining power of the Church in post-Renaissance Europe, which paved the way to the modern age.

The new impetus to the pursuit of knowledge that was such a significant development in Greece had an increasing influence on astrology when the emperor Alexander conquered Mesopotamia in 331 BC. Now there was an exciting intermingling of different cultural traditions, of ancient wisdom systems and new, protoscientific developments. It is during this period that we see astronomy and astrology, the science of celestial measurement and the art of its interpretation, which were not yet distinct from one another, take a quantum leap.

The compilation of planetary tables made possible as never before the composition of written astrological charts set up for a given moment. By this time the zodiac circle of twelve constellations had long been known, and this was now refined into a system of twelve signs of equal size. The mapping of the entire sky at a particular time of day involved the determination and eventual interpretation of the ascendant, from which the system of houses developed. Whereas in earlier days only the conjunction and opposition of planets had been considered, greater precision of measurement led to the consideration of other kinds of planetary relationships. By the beginning of the Christian era, the foundations of astrology as it is now practised in the West had been laid.

At some much earlier point, as I have suggested above, the sign-reading out of which astrology grew had probably undergone a shift from pure association to an attribution of divine causation. Now another dramatic development was taking place. Instead of gazing at the sky and being awe-struck by the visible indications of divine will, it was now possible, without a particular religious framework, to ascertain from tables the predetermined positions of planets moving according to orderly principles and to use these abstractions as a basis for interpretation. It was possible, in fact, to see the whole process as the predictable working out of natural physical laws, like the cycle of seasons or the phases of the moon, and to see these natural processes, rather than divine caprice, as the cause of what befell humanity. In short, it was possible to understand astrology not in magical or religious terms, but scientifically, for now a process of differentiation was taking place between religious belief and natural science. Although these different explanations are not necessarily mutually exclusive and often overlap, something of a split had developed between irrational and inductive interpretations on the one hand and rational and deductive interpretations on the other. Scientific astrology was developed particularly by the Stoic philosophers, followed by the influential Ptolemy, but the magical view could not be banished. The split between the two views has continued to characterise astrology.

A further consequence of the possibility of detailed chart erection, combined with a developing interest in individual as opposed to collective destiny, was the emergence of natal astrology, the use of the individual birth chart. The earliest one known today dates from the end of the fifth century BC.

Another possibility inherent in a chart based on accurate calculation is its systematic projection into the future via the continuing and predeterminable cyclic motions of the planets. In other words, a basis for the development of transits and progressions (see Chapter 6) now existed.

Astrology continued to develop alongside mathematics and astronomy in Greece and Rome, in Alexandria in Egypt, and later in the new Islamic culture whose centre for a long time was the Mesopotamian city of Baghdad. The Arabs adopted the Indian counting system, on which the numerals we use today are based and which, particularly on account of the figure zero (a feature lacking in Greek and Roman counting systems), greatly facilitated calculations. They continued to develop a highly mathematical astrology which spread to Europe during the Middle Ages, while in other cultures such as China, which developed its own separate astrological system, the actual appearances of phenomena in the sky continued to be an important consideration. As late as the seventeenth century AD, Johannes Kepler, one of the last official astrologers and a founder of the modern science of astronomy, was known by the title of *mathematicus*, mathematician, in his rule as court astrologer to Emperor Rudolf II in Prague.

Let us take a leap now to the present day and consider some of the ways in which modern astrologers view the nature of their art, in which the elements of magic, religion and natural science are still fundamental.

The principle of causality is a dominant feature of the Western tradition, whether God is regarded as the ultimate cause or dispensed with entirely and replaced by natural laws. One of the ancient teachers upon whose work Western astrology has been based, Claudius Ptolemy, who lived in Egypt in the second century of our era, emphasised the analogy between astrology and the sorts of natural cycles which any peasant may observe. This notion that the planets themselves in their cycles, with or without a god behind them, have a direct effect on earthly goings-on, has tended to be favoured. Many modern textbooks on astrology still speak in terms of the *influence* of the heavenly bodies, and in fact the word "influence" itself derives from the belief that some kind of energy *flows in* on us from the skies.

Recent research on the effects of the lunar cycles on human and animal behaviour and plant growth[8] encourages the thought that the phases of the planetary cycles may also have physically measurable effects, and some research has been carried out which may demonstrate that certain interplanetary angles (aspects) affect certain chemical experiments[9]. This research is not conclusive, but it is a well-known phenomenon that chemical experiments in general are prone to mysterious failures and inconsistencies at times. Other scientists have attempted to find mechanisms through which celestial influences could operate, and tend to focus on electro-magnetic and gravitational forces. One scientific researcher has suggested that the physiological organ through which such influences enter is the pineal gland[10]. This light-sensitive organ which produces a biochemical reaction could conceivably set in motion a complex of biorhythms on its first exposure to light and other influences.

The problem with the causal explanation is that, though it may explain some features of astrology, it can scarcely be stretched comfortably to cover all. When a horary chart is cast the only causality we can readily imagine is this: that the quality of the influences at that moment causes the question to be asked at this time rather than another. The events to which the chart relates, which may lie in the past or future, can hardly be said to be caused by that planetary pattern. And even in natal astrology causal theory runs into difficulties. We can understand that *transits*, that is, the current positions of the planets at some moment after birth interacting with the original birth horoscope, may have an effect by stimulating the natal pattern, but *progressions*, which are also used to predict developments, are derived from the natal chart without any basis in current actuality.

The principle of cause and effect, the basis of classical science, is so deeply embedded in our language and way of thinking that it is difficult to describe phenomena, including astrological phenomena, in any other terms. We read or hear that the sun in Leo *makes* people regal and self-important, or that a transit *triggers off* a configuration on the birth chart. This presupposes a sequence. Let us suppose—and it often is supposed—that at birth the infant is exposed to the influence of the heavenly configurations, that a pattern of rays or energies from the planets and signs is stamped on the newborn child and the effects of this operation are experienced throughout his or her life. It would be difficult to imagine that the planetary pattern at death retrospectively influenced that individual's character and destiny, because we inevitably think of causes as preceding effects.

Logicians have often pointed out that because one thing follows another it does not necessarily mean that the second is caused by the first (*post quod* does not necessarily mean *propter quod*), but we do assume that effects follow causes (*propter quod* necessarily means *post quod*). In quantum physics, however, which in many respects challenges the bases of classical science[11], causes can follow effects, making a nonsense of our notions of causality. Now once again it becomes possible to question the universal validity of the law of cause and effect which, as we have seen, has not always and everywhere dominated the human mind.

The possibility of the existence of an *acausal connecting principle* has been put forward by the great Swiss psychologist C.G. Jung. He called this principle *synchronicity*, or meaningful coincidence. His ideas on the nature of synchronicity developed and changed over time, remaining rather mysterious, but basically he recognised the possibility that two or more occurrences, often close together in time, could be related in *meaning* without having any sort of causal link. To give an example from my own experience, I once had a dream which involved a little girl with blond, curly hair called Chloe. The dream was a highly significant one for me: important inner changes were reflected in the dream by the birth of the little girl, who rapidly developed to the age of about three or four. The mythological dimensions of the name Chloe were also an important feature of the dream. I had only ever known one person with this name, years before. The following day I was standing at a bus-stop when I was approached by a little girl of about four with blond, curly hair, and a brief interaction developed. When the bus came the mother summoned the child, addressing her by the name of Chloe. A coincidence, to be sure, but a coincidence charged with significance for me. The normal boundary between inner realities and external phenomena appeared somehow to have broken down.

We tend to assume that the law of cause and effect operates in an absolute manner, regardless of our subjective involvement, but this assumption too has been questioned in the light of the strange phenomena of quantum physics. It is now licit to view causality as having the status of a theory, and one which does not explain all known phenomena. We may dare to consider the possibility that causality exists only in the mind that perceives it. With synchronicity, complete objectivity is usually ruled out from the start, as *meaning* is involved and there must be a mind to attribute a meaning to the phenomenon. My meeting with the child at the bus-stop was only meaningful because of the power of my subjective interpretation of dream and meeting; otherwise it would have been merely a coincidence, or perhaps a trivial instance of precognition.

In relation to astrology the principle of acausality also has a pedigree, alongside the theory of influence. It exists in the ancient principle of correspondences, succinctly defined in the adage "as above, so below", from a highly influential Arabic text attributed to Hermes Trismegistus (Thrice-Great Hermes), who was also identified with the Egyptian god Thoth. All divinatory phenomena can be understood in terms of correspondence. This involves the assumption that all phenomena are interrelated so that, if we only know how to look, we can determine the nature and direction of any part of the universal process by carefully examining another part. According to the principle of correspondences, all phenomena can be grouped into families of related meaning, and specifically, every animal, vegetable or mineral item belongs to the family or category headed by one of the planets. Thus Mars, the hot, fiery planet, associated with the use of the sword, rules iron, from which weapons have been made since its discovery, anything sharp, and hot-tasting or burning plants such as the onion and stinging nettle. The fascinating thing about these traditional intuitive associations is that more recent discoveries have often tended to support them. Gold, for example, long associated with the heart, when found within the human body (it has been and still sometimes is ingested for medicinal purposes) tends to concentrate in the region of the heart. Copper and iron, the metals of Venus and Mars, occur in different ratios in the blood serum of the two sexes, with a preponderance of copper (corresponding to the feminine planet) in the case of women, and of iron in the case of men. The two metals are also found together in the earth[9]. In mythology Venus and Mars (Aphrodite and Ares) were lovers, and in astrology they form a masculine/feminine pair. Scientific findings suggest that these correspondences have some objective reality.

The idea that by looking at one part of the universe (that is, the planets) we may learn something about another part is a variation of the idea that the whole of reality is somehow contained in any part, the universe in a grain of sand, the macrocosm in the microcosm. An analogy can be drawn with holography. The hologram is a three-dimensional image produced by means of lasers, and any fragment of a holographic plate contains and reproduces the whole image.

Can it be said that the nature of the time is always reflected in the current celestial picture, and that anything born at that moment is imbued with the moment's qualities? Perhaps. Certainly there are such things as the spirit of the time, and ideas, discoveries and inventions whose moment has come. There is, however, no real *evidence* that this is what astrology is about, although the experience of astrologers constantly seems to confirm this view. It certainly appears *as if* astrology participates in a continuing process of correspondence, and the idea that the universe is one, and all beings and phenomena inter-connected parts of the same process, is not only of considerable antiquity but also has its counterpart in reports of mystical experiences of widely differing traditions, and of certain drug-induced states of mind, and has recently popped up again in the *avant garde* of modern physics. Professor of Theoretical Physics, David Bohm has proposed[12] the existence of what he calls the "implicate" or "folded-in" order, an order everywhere and always present in a universe which is an undivided whole, and which can at any point be unfolded. Astrology appears to point towards an order lying hidden in the heart of all existence.

Another way in which we might conceive of astrology as working is to deny any *objective* reality to astrological phenomena at all and say that it is purely a question of what the intuitive eye of the astrologer sees in the chart. We might imagine that by some psychic means, potentially accessible perhaps to all of us, the astrologer *knows* already what she is looking for in the chart and the chart is simply a tool which amplifies this intuitive perception. This would mean that there is really no connection between a horoscope based on the time of birth and the individual whom it represents. We could, in effect, if we wished to change ourselves, simply adopt a different chart. The experience of most astrologers, however, from their own charts as much as the charts of others, is that the chart usually seems inescapably bound up with the fate of the individual and, moreover, that it is often possible to deduce certain features of an individual's chart from knowing the person, on the basis of past astrological experience.

It may be that research will eventually make clear what kind of phenomenon we are dealing with in astrology, either soon or at some point when our understanding has enlarged sufficiently to grasp new principles. In recent years a number of scientists have set out to examine astrology, but the results have often served to perplex us further. Many of the experiments, including those which claim to have "disproved" astrology, have been badly designed, the problem often being the hidden assumptions of the experimenters. "Objective" science, which we have been schooled into seeing as the embodiment of truth, may also be viewed as a set of beliefs, a religion whose rituals are performed by priests in white coats, and some of the basic assumptions of scientists in the past are now being questioned by scientists themselves. In fact, some of the phenomena uncovered by twentieth-century physics and mathematics are so odd and apparently irrational as to make astrology seem not so queer after all. Stranger things have been observed in laboratories. In particular, the discovery that in quantum physics the observer is part of the experiment challenges the basic assumption of scientific objectivity. Many of those investigating astrology scientifically will only accept it if it can be shown to be completely objective, which a system involving symbolic meanings can scarcely be, and if it can be understood in over-simple causal terms. This may prove to be a blind alley in understanding astrology, as indeed it seems to be in understanding the sub-atomic world.

The biggest and best-known scientific investigations of astrology to date have been those of the French statistician Michel Gauquelin, who began with the intention of disproving astrology and ended up rediscovering it in his own terms. His findings, based on the birth charts of very large numbers of individuals eminent in certain fields, such as scientists or sportsmen, showed a distinct correlation between each profession and the positions of particular planets, mainly those planets which traditional astrology already associated with such callings. But, curiously, the positions of these planets did not quite fit the traditional expectations. For example, on most of the scientists' charts, Saturn fell just inside the ninth and twelfth houses rather than just over the cusp in the tenth and first, which is where astrologers would expect. What is more, although further studies on eminent people continued to fit the pattern of earlier experiments, Gauquelin was unable to replicate his results using charts of ordinary people. This may lead us into all kinds of speculations and reflections, such as the recollection that astrology was originally used only for prominent people, that is to say kings, but it certainly complicates the issue rather than simplifying it and does little to explain astrology as it is generally practised.

Perhaps there is a fundamental flaw in looking for scientific explanations as an alternative to magical or religious ones. Remember that at an earlier stage in the evolution of human consciousness such distinctions were not made. Perhaps it is possible to arrive at some kind of holistic view in which science and magic are not seen as altogether contradictory. From a psychological point of view it may be said that a certain type of individual perceives and describes the world in scientific terms while another, differently orientated, perceives the same reality intuitively. Symbolically we might describe the former as a solar and the latter as a lunar attitude. Interestingly, the Babylonians, whose astrology might be characterised as more intuitive, considered the moon of greater importance, corresponding to an important deity, while in the more rationally orientated Roman world sun-worship became the major religion and the sun was accorded greater significance in astrology.

I do not feel that either of these attitudes tells the whole story, either of astrology or of the cosmos. We cannot revert to a purely magical world-view in which the intuitive and the scientific are not differentiated, but perhaps we can hope to reach a new level of consciousness where the two can be seen as complementary, and arrive at a new kind of synthesis. It may even be that astrology itself holds a key to healing the split between rational and irrational, matter and mind, objective and subjective.

Chapter 4

Astrology and Psychology

Psychology is literally the study of psyche, but what do we mean by psyche? When we talk about the human body we feel we know what we are dealing with; it can be apprehended by the senses and measured, we can point to different parts of it and name them, confident that others will understand what we mean by "head" or "heart" as anatomical items, though these same terms have less obvious, metaphorical meanings as well. When we try to describe the non-physical aspects of the human being, or for that matter of other animals, we are getting into territory much more difficult to chart. It is understandable that the modern *science* of psychology (psychology is not necessarily to be classified as a science) chooses not to indulge in too much speculation on the nature of invisible psychic operations but rather to deal with their effects in the form of behaviour, which can be observed and measured.

To the ancients the non-physical entity inhabiting the body was often symbolised by breath. The moment of birth for astrological purposes is often timed by the first independent breath, and death occurs when we "breathe our last". The soul or psyche was sometimes depicted in antiquity as a butterfly leaving the lips of the dying person. Breath was that which *animated* the body, and the Latin word *anima*, usually translated as *soul*, comes from a root meaning breath and is related to the Sanskrit *atman*, usually rendered as *self*. *Spirit* comes from Latin *spirare*, to breathe, and *psyche* from a Greek word also meaning to breathe. So psychology is the study of that invisible, animating power in us whose metaphor is breath and whose nature is still mysterious.

The word for body is simple and straightforward. We all think we know what that is. But what do we mean by mind, spirit, soul, self, to say nothing of instincts, feelings and intuitions? Does soul mean the same thing to a Christian as it did to Pythagoras? When we use the word "mind" do we mean intellect or something broader? Do we have a spirit in addition to a soul? Is ego the same thing as self or a feeling the same thing as an emotion? How we define any of these terms depends on the particular framework we use; we are dealing with extremely elusive concepts, and it is on these that we have to base any explanation of individual differences in character and behaviour.

The word *psychologia* was originally coined in the context of Christian philosophy in the fifteenth century and meant the study of the soul. At that time all orthodox pursuit of knowledge was carried out under the auspices of the Christian Church, out of whose educational function the universities had developed. But by the fifteenth century the central authority of the Church was already beginning to be challenged, leading to the Reformation. The invention of the printing press made educational material more available. In the seventeenth and eighteenth centuries came what has been called the "Enlightenment", a period in which the pursuit of knowledge was secularised; this was the beginning of what we now call science.

It was during this period that psychology in the modern sense of the word came into being—a new secular study of the non-physical aspect of people which no longer needed to be described in terms of the theological view of the soul. By today the term has developed in numerous directions. It means different things to different people—the study of mind, feelings, inner processes, behaviour, carried out in a variety of ways. It means something different to an experimental researcher, to a psychiatrist (who has a medical training), to psychotherapists of various complexions attempting to understand and heal psychological dis-ease.

It is not possible in this book to do justice to the variety of psychological schools in existence, but two points are worth stressing. The first is that in whichever way we define the subject of psychology, it has been studied more systematically and in greater depth during the last century than ever before, and techniques of psychotherapy have correspondingly developed beyond anything hitherto known. Secondly, the concepts of these new areas of study have been steadily filtering through to the population at large, becoming part of the cultural background. Many psychological theories and concepts have slipped into our thoughts and speech (Freudian slip, complex, repression, introvert/extrovert, I.Q.); we find psychological articles in magazines ("Are you a considerate partner?"); we are offered psychological insights and advice on radio and television, we watch psychological movies. During the twentieth century psychology has worked itself well into our consciousness and the modern astrological revival owes much to this development.

Although earlier centuries had no concept of psychology, people nonetheless grappled with many issues which we now group under that heading, questions concerning psychic anatomy (mind, spirit, intellect, etc), questions about how people came to have certain characteristics, why they behaved as they did, how they were drawn to particular circumstances. In ancient Greece, a major source of our cultural tradition and probably the birthplace of natal astrology, although people were on one level held responsible for their own actions, the powers that motivated them were generally described in terms that suggested that they controlled the individual rather than vice versa. Fate, for a start, might decree the qualities allotted to a person, or he might be influenced by forces or entities which irrupted into his life, usually at the instigation of a god. The same sort of notion is conveyed by such expressions as "I was seized by rage" or "the spirit moved me". Protective and malevolent spirits and the shades of the dead were evoked to explain why a person was happy or unhappy, and indeed these may still be considered to exert psychological influence.

By the time astrology caught on in Greece, the gods were becoming less real to people, and a more secular spirit of enquiry was developing, the beginnings of scientific exploration. The study of medicine as it developed in the wake of Hippocrates in the sixth century BC provided a different explanation of individual characteristics and behaviour from that based on divine interventions and mysterious forces. Hippocrates is reputed to have judged even moral disposition from the pulse, and out of such theories grew the study of physiognomy, according to which character was deduced by judgement of physiological characteristics, particularly the features and irregularities of head and face. While physiognomy may sometimes have been understood in terms of *correspondence* between the physical and psychological, the medical tradition, particularly from the time of Galen, whose system was the basis of European medicine until the modern era, tended to see the relationship as causal: the idiosyncrasies of the body, itself influenced by the environment, were seen as the causes of all psychological conditions. Alongside this medical approach, belief in the moral and spiritual causes of psychological disturbance, and in interference by demons and other non-physical influences continued. Just as secular, "scientific" astrology came to compete with "magical" or religious astrology, so the same split developed in the study of the nature of individual men and women. As these two trends in astrology have continued to the present time, so have the different approaches to the human psyche, with some theorists, notably the medical profession, seeking and perceiving causes for psychological conditions in biology, while others explain the same conditions in terms of intangible psychological forces which inhabit and interact with, but are not necessarily produced by, the body.

A major aspect of Hippocratic medicine that was to influence astrology was his system of four *humours* or bodily fluids, which was later to be developed by Galen. While everybody had these four fluids, they were believed to be mixed in different proportions in different individuals, and as no individual was in perfect balance, each was deemed to have one humour predominating, and this determined his *temperament*. The four types were the *sanguine*, in whom blood predominated, the *choleric*, with a predominance of choler or bile, the *phlegmatic*, with a preponderance of phlegm, and the *melancholic*, or black bile type. The balance was also modified by seasons and environmental conditions, and serious imbalances led to illness. Each temperament had its particular psychological as well as physical qualities.

The notion that people were made up of four *elements* (earth, air, fire, water), which was to merge with humoral theory, had a separate origin in the teachings of another great teacher of the fertile sixth century BC, Pythagoras. First it was observed that the universe was composed of these four elements (we might call them the solid, gaseous, incandescent and liquid states of matter), and this led to the assumption that each individual was also composed of these (body solids and fluids, warmth and air). Eventually a system developed according to which each of the four temperaments with its predominant humour was regarded as corresponding to one of the four elements. The sanguine (blood) was the airy type, the choleric (bile) the fiery type, the phlegmatic (phlegm) the watery type and the melancholic (black bile) the earthy type. Although the perception of the exact nature of each type went through modifications in the course of time, the system of humours and temperaments held sway for over a thousand years, and there are still traces of it in some modern psychological systems[13].

When astrology first became integrated into humoral medicine, the four elements were not related to the four sets of zodiacal signs as they are today, but to the planets, and there are some surprises here for the modern astrologer. As we would expect, the sun and Mars were usually considered to be fiery in nature, and the moon watery, and Saturn was always felt to be earthy. Less obvious to us is the usual medieval identification of Venus as a watery and Jupiter as an airy planet. Mercury was always considered neutral, able to take on the characteristics of any element. Later, complex rules were developed for determining the temperament from the natal chart. Seventeenth-century astrologer and herbalist Nicholas Culpeper wrote some particularly colourful descriptions of the four temperaments. For him the choleric type was "quick-witted, bold, unshamefac'd, furious, hasty, quarrelsom, irefull, fraudulent, stout, arrogant, couragious, gracelesse, cruel, crafty, and unconstant"; phlegmatics were "dull, heavy, sloathful, sleepy, cowardish, fearful, covetous, self-lovers, slow of motion, shamefac'd, and sober"; melancholics were "covetous, selfelovers, fearfull without cause, pusillanimous, solitary, careful, lumpish, seldome merry or laughing, stout, stubborn, ambitious, envious, fretful, obstinate in opinions, of a deep cogitation, mistrustful, suspicious, vexed with dolours of the mind, and dreadful imaginations, (as though they were infested with evil spirits) and ... very spightful, curious, squeamish, and yet slovens, high-minded, and very majestical in behaviour, and retain[ed] their anger long". So far, so bad. But of the sanguine (airy) type Culpeper reports that he is "merry, liberal, bountiful, merciful, courteous, bold enough, trusty, faithful and of good behaviour".

Blood, the humour predominating in the sanguine type,

had of course more positive associations than phlegm, bile and black bile, blood being so obviously essential for life, and air was associated with the heaven above where God was imagined to reign. On the traditional diagram, earth and air were opposite each other, which meant that Saturn, known as the Great Malefic, was opposed by Jupiter, the Great Benefic. The antagonism between them was the pull between earth and heaven, and in Christian terms they tended to line up with the godly (Jupiter) and the devilish (Saturn — matter, flesh) in that spirit/matter split which has characterised our culture. The sanguine or airy temperament associated with Jupiter was the one that came to be described in glowing terms, while of the melancholic little good was said. Sometimes air was associated particularly with man as opposed to the animal realm, man alone being supposed to have the privilege of a divine soul. We see this also in the figures that go with the airy signs of the zodiac: there are no animals here, but in two cases human beings (Aquarius, the water-bearer, and Gemini, the twins) and in the remaining one (Libra, the scales) a product of human ingenuity.

Here we come to a crucial point in the difference between natal astrology as practised before the Enlightenment and as newly discovered after the development of modern psychology. In the earlier form suffering and evil coalesced, and as the experience of Saturn was recognised as bringing difficulties and a sense of limitation and being bound by the flesh, there was a tendency to evaluate his influence on human nature in terms of evil characteristics. Where Jupiter was strong on a natal chart flattering descriptions tended to be lavished. While there are still astrologers who believe that they are in a position to make moral judgements on those whose charts they read, the modern, more psychological tendency is to drop the words good and evil in favour of terms like easy and difficult. The individual with a strong Jupiter tends to feel better about herself, buoyant, expecting the best, refusing to acknowledge limitations, while the Saturnian type is on the whole more pessimistic, reserved and conscious of proper form. Though the Jupiterian type is more likely to be good at making friends and influencing people this does not necessarily mean that he or she is of high moral character — many criminals, and most of the top Nazis, have charts with a strong Jupiterian influence.

In traditional astrology judgement of character was far from being the most important issue. Much attention was paid to physical constitution and appearance, and to health. The kinds of people the native (i.e. the person for whom the birth chart or *nativity* was cast) was likely to come into contact with were also the objects of much deliberation, as the attributes of the houses show: marriage partner, siblings, children, friends, and so forth. Then there was the question of profession, and the all-important one of wealth or lack of it, the likelihood of travel, of events of various kinds, and the type of death to be expected. All of these matters were considered as *happening to* the native and to have little connection with the psyche. Ptolemy includes in the *Tetrabiblos* a chapter on the quality of the soul (*psyche* in the original Greek); the soul is governed in principle by two planets only, Mercury (the rational part) and the moon (irrational), although much of course depends on the signs involved˙ and the influences on these two from other planets, and Ptolemy recognises that he is dealing with a complex issue. Fifteen hundred years later Lilly relates the same two planets to what he calls wit and intellect, that is to say, he puts the emphasis on mind rather than soul, and he includes a separate section on "manners", of which a particular planet will be the significator on a given chart.

One of the very big changes brought to astrology by modern psychology, and in particular by the theories attendant on psychotherapy, is the recognition that many of the experiences and events in our lives, including those pertaining to our health, to say nothing of the kind of people we attract as friends, enemies or partners, are drawn to us by our own qualities, attitudes and needs, that these are in some way responsible for the form our lives take. It is not an entirely new idea; in the sixth century BC Heraclitus had already affirmed that character is destiny, but it is only recently that the full implications of this perception for natal interpretation have been realised. Once one has really looked into the way that we create the situations we find ourselves in, one is compelled to read the astrological symbolism in a rather different way — granted that there are people for whom all of this is a closed door, and whose astrological interpretation is therefore not markedly different from that practised three centuries ago.

One of the biggest differences between these two approaches results from the idea of unconscious or subconscious psychic activity — and the assumption that such a thing exists has crept into popular thought. Supposing I walk off with your book. Now I could say, "I did it accidentally". Fair enough, perhaps, but if I told that to my psychotherapist I would probably be encouraged to question how much accident was actually involved. If I say, "I did it unconsciously", there is quite a different implication, an implication of some sort of responsibility on my part. The possibility is suggested that I might have had some hidden motive in taking your book, hidden even from myself. Perhaps I simply wanted to read the book but didn't feel able to ask to borrow it. Or perhaps the fact that the book is *yours* is the crucial factor: by taking it I take a bit of you with me, and may well ensure that I have further contact with you, a reason to telephone you or call to bring it back. Nearly always, the "accidents" of our lives turn out to look less accidental when we look at the meaning they have for us, and what we gain or lose from them. The word that "accidentally" slips out is a familiar example to most of us. If I leave your house after dinner with the words, "Thank you for the hostility", you may rightly conclude that there is something other in my attitude than the politeness and gratitude I am trying to convey.

The idea that we are responsible for the things that "happen to" us has profound implications. One is the possibility that if I am responsible for these things there should be something I can do to change them. I can begin to recognise patterns in these "accidents", to get in touch with aspects of myself I was earlier unaware of, and in so doing I get a little more control over them. The woman who keeps being attracted to men who, though charming on first meeting, invariably turn out to be violent, may begin to see that there is a level on which she is picking up and actually choosing the violence. If she can understand what prompts her to do that, she has the possibility of breaking the pattern so that she no longer winds up bruised and bitter. This means that we are bound to reconsider what traditional astrologers had to say about the marriage partner. They seemed to imply that it was somehow decreed by external factors that a man would marry a certain type of woman, whereas now many people would agree that it was something inside him that decreed the choice, even of those aspects of her which he did not consciously recognise when he met her. We might even say that he chooses her because she fits some sort of inner picture of a woman that he carries round inside him, much of it unconscious. Instead of reading into a chart that a man will marry a particular kind of woman, we will then see that he is likely to be drawn to certain qualities in a partner, and the more aware he is of this, the more choice he will have and the better able he will be to avoid attracting the worst possible manifestations of the birth chart partner.

There is an obvious sense in which a man, and more particularly a woman, has more choice as to whom he or she marries today than was the case in the nineteenth century when astrology was last widely practised. In fact, the increased choice and responsibility that result from psychological insights now available to us parallel an increase in choice and responsibility of a more obvious kind that has developed in Western society over the last two or three hundred years. A butcher's son no longer feels that he must automatically become a butcher, and a woman no longer feels she must confine her activities to the home. The greater availability of information, made possible by modern communications media, dangles before us possibilities that our great-grandparents never imagined, and new means of travel have greatly increased our potential field of activities. We can also tamper with nature as never before.

The secularisation of education and knowledge is a key factor in these developments, granting us extraordinary powers we had hitherto accepted as the prerogative of a transcendental God, and along with them huge responsibilities which we seem ill-equipped to handle, as the development of nuclear physics and the Pandora's box of the chemical and biochemical industries illustrate. Even psychological understanding creates new possibilities for destructive manipulations, in the torture chamber as in subtler interactions.

Arguably, however, employing psychology to understand our individual motivations and inner conflicts could be the decisive factor in making wise use of our vastly increased powers, for behind all the supposedly "objective" findings of science, and behind all political and economic processes and military conflicts, stand individuals making judgements and decisions, relying to a considerable extent on personal motivations, subjective impressions and hidden assumptions and beliefs. If we really want to change the world for the better, we must start with ourselves and examine the processes that go on within us and between us.

So the Western world has changed quite radically since the days of Lilly and Culpeper: not only has our environment changed dramatically but we do not see it through the same eyes as they did. In particular, the study of psychology or the experience of psychotherapy changes our perceptions of ourselves and of others, and few of us have been completely untouched by these new developments. If we approach astrology permeated with such influences we necessarily see it in a rather different framework from our predecessors. From a psychological standpoint, "psyche" cannot be represented on the birth chart by one or two planets only, but pervades the whole, because it pervades all the issues the chart speaks of: home, career, finances, friendships, health, the timing of events, and all those issues people have always consulted astrologers about.

To take health as an example: while our health is undoubtedly affected by external factors beyond our control, psychological factors are increasingly recognised as playing an important role. Even the common cold is stress-related, and people often get ill because they need a rest, or need to be looked after. The great early twentieth-century astrologer Charles Carter, who was in fact concerned to incorporate the new ideas of psychology into his work, remarks in a book first published in 1930[14] that individuals with stressful connections between the moon and Mars on their birth chart may be either pugnacious and combative or inclined to ill health. Fifty to sixty years after he wrote this, these alternative modes of expression of moon/Mars combinations may readily be seen as two sides of the same coin, since it is now a commonplace that when anger and aggression are denied they are likely to turn inwards and undermine health. The profile of the "cancer-prone personality", for example, is well-known to feature an inability to express anger.

Nor are events that surprise us and change our lives necessarily separate from psychology. If a man loses all his money or a woman inadvertently becomes pregnant, it is pertinent to ask what was going on inside them that they came to such a pass, and as astrology inevitably responds to us in the manner in which we approach it, it can give us psychological answers, or at least clues, to such psychological questions. There are of course events in our lives which we cannot be held responsible for; it is inevitable, for example, that our parents will die at some point, and very likely during our own lives, and we would expect to find such events mirrored in the birth chart. Other kinds of events, too, will have their astrological counterparts where any theory of personal responsibility seems too far-fetched. The relationship between the inner and outer worlds is mysterious, and astrology constantly causes us to blink at the way the two fit and belong together, as if they are aspects of one system. However an event comes about, we can pick up a good deal from the chart about the nature of its impact on us, for it is inevitable that it will have psychological implications and be meaningfully woven into our life pattern.

This does not mean that planetary symbols are simply to be equated with psychological forces; an astrological chart can be meaningful in very different ways — it may refer to a business launch, a lost cow or a potential harvest rather than to a person — but what it does mean is that these ancient symbols can be related to the flora and fauna of the psychological landscape, just as they can to those which inhabit the earth's surface.

Earlier in this chapter I suggested that the ancient Greeks had at least two approaches to explaining psychological phenomena, one rationally based (the medical model), and one irrationally based (mysterious, autonomous forces affecting the individual). There also existed, however, what is sometimes seen today as a much more fully developed ancient psychology embodied in the myths handed on from generation to generation, in the patterns of events described and in the capricious behaviour of the gods and goddesses, after some of whom our planets are named. C.G. Jung first expressed the view that mythology was nothing less than the psychology of antiquity, and that the ancient gods are still alive and well and operative in our lives, and still worthy of our respect. Bearing this in mind, it can be extremely enriching and illuminating to explore the myths associated with the gods who feature on the birth chart, and with the images that belong to the signs.

The planets are now known to us by the Latin names corresponding to those of the gods of ancient Greece, and the Greeks in turn had given the planets the names of those gods which most nearly corresponded to the Babylonian gods whose names they already bore. There are abundant qualities associated with the astrological meanings of the planets which we find reflected in the corresponding myths, and the myths can enlarge our understanding of them. Mercury (Hermes in Greek) was the messenger of the gods, and also the god of merchants, hence associated with the principle of exchange. The function of the planet relates to the process of giving and receiving information and of exchange on all levels, and in particular with language. He was also the god of thieves, a liar and mischief-maker, an adept at the crooked bargain. On the first day of his life (he was also precocious!) he left his cradle, and after killing a tortoise and turning its shell into a lyre, he stole fifty cows from one of his half-brother Apollo's herds by making them walk backwards and wiping over their tracks with twigs. Having eaten his fill of beef and offered a sacrifice he returned home. Apollo, who had been informed of Hermes' antics, was exceedingly angry with the child, but Hermes, never at a loss for a cheeky word, assured his victim that he didn't even know the meaning of the word "cow". Hauled up before Zeus, the king of the gods, Hermes eventually agreed to return the remainder of the cattle, but in the meantime had stolen Apollo's bow and arrows. To placate his brother, Hermes next offered him the tortoise-shell lyre, flattering him about his musical talents, in exchange being given further gifts and powers by Apollo.

The qualities demonstrated by Hermes in this story, a

quick tongue, skill at sleights of hand and the ability to do a smart deal, tend to be evident in people with Mercury prominent on their charts. But we need not confine ourselves to Greek myths: there are figures and stories from other traditions that we might link to the functions of the astrological symbols. We could, in relation to Mercury, dip into the stories about the Scandinavian god Loki, whose amorality and mischievousness connect him with Mercury's trickster role; or about the wise Egyptian Thoth, whose invention of writing can be associated with the Mercurial function of message-bearing. In this way we can accumulate a series of overlapping pictures which describe activities related to the planet as they have been perceived in the past, in our own and related cultures. For we have not sprung from nowhere — we are the products of millions of years of evolution and thousands of years of tradition, and this is as true of our inner life as it is of our external achievements. Myths hand on important elements of our outer, but more especially of our inner history.

The psychologically-orientated astrologer approaches the old problems in a new way, and very likely will not wish to try to answer such questions as "Will I get rich?" Of what use, then, is this new kind of astrology? Its value as a tool for psychological insights is considerable. It can bring to our attention aspects of ourselves we were unaware of, resources we did not know we possessed, options we had not considered. It can help us figure out what it is we do wrong, how we get ourselves into familiar situations and how we might go about things differently. It can provide a framework within which to view our lives, and it can help us see the meaning in experiences we would otherwise have dismissed. The birth chart can in fact be a companion with which we can dialogue when we wish to understand ourselves better, a mirror in which we can see constantly changing images of ourselves. Astrology is probably more available than ever before to individuals who want not so much to get a few cut-and-dried answers from an astrologer but to explore the subject for themselves and use the horoscope as an aid to personal growth.

Any kind of psychological approach to astrology involves an attempt to understand the causes and consequences of the processes indicated by the astrological symbolism, or at least to connect the experiences they correspond to back to the individual who experiences them, and to make sense of them in terms of the life process. To what degree we bring particular psychological models to astrology is a matter of personal choice. Among psychological theorists, Jung's emphasis on the symbolic dimension and on myths has made him something of a favourite among astrologers, and he has very much coloured my own approach, but astrology itself is neutral in this respect, and will respond to us in the manner in which we approach it, always able to absorb and adapt, to a greater or lesser degree, to different theories about the way human beings function, of which no doubt there are many more to come. If it is a useless theory, astrology will not make it any more useful, but in any case astrology can give it another dimension. Of course it will not be found that one psychological term can simply be translated into a single astrological one, or vice versa, but it will always be possible for a psychology and its variables to be described in astrological terms. It is not a question of imposing on astrology the straightjacket of a particular school of psychological thought, but of constantly rediscovering it in the light of new ideas. There is no such thing as "pure astrology"; it only exists when applied to something, and human nature, a commodity always amenable to new insights, remains an area of application as vital as any.

Chapter 5

The Birth Chart

Planets and Signs

The planets, and in astrology this term includes the "lights", the sun and moon, are the characters in the personal drama of the birth chart. Traditionally there were seven planets (three plus four) on the background of the twelve signs (three times four). Each sign was associated with, or *ruled* by a planet, the sun and moon ruling one sign each (Leo and Cancer) and the remainder each ruling two signs, in the symmetrical pattern shown in Figure 4.

SUN AND MOON

One of the earliest distinctions appears to have been that between masculine and feminine planets, appropriate to the genders of the deities after whom they were named. When considering the chart as a psychological map it is important to have some understanding of the meaning of this polarity. Like the gods and goddesses, the significant figures that appear in our dreams, and which many psychotherapists would understand as representing aspects of ourselves, can usually first of all be classified as either male or female. Just as dream figures of whichever sex can be interpreted as parts of ourselves, and as the gods and goddesses can be understood as principles at work within each of us, to which the mythologising mind has intuitively given masculine or feminine gender, so do we each have a full complement of masculine and feminine factors on our birth chart. In each

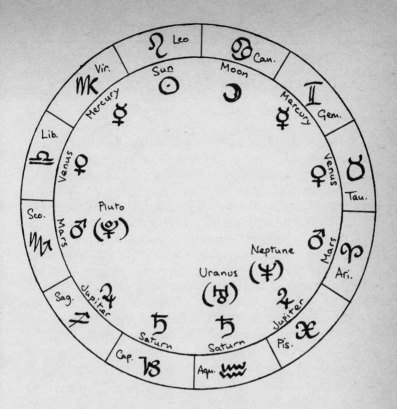

Figure 4   Signs with rulers (new planets in brackets)

of us, that is to say, there is a balance of the masculine and feminine principles, although we may expect that, by and large, women will develop more strongly those characteristics associated with the feminine planets and men those associated with the masculine planets.

This fundamental polarity is not an absolute and rigid distinction. It corresponds roughly to the Chinese yin and yang, which originally referred to the shadowy and the bright sides of a mountain. The underlying notion is that all phenomena come into being through the interplay of opposites, that what was originally one, undifferentiated, becomes two, and from the permutations of these multiplicity develops, and that every situation can be defined in terms of yin/yang balance. The yang or masculine tends to be identified with the active, the bright, the rational, and heaven above, and the yin or feminine with the passive or receptive, the dark, the irrational and the earth below. The signs of the zodiac are often divided into positive and negative, like electromagnetic poles, but it is the same yang/yin distinction. If some of the attributes of the "masculine" tend to imply "superiority", such as positive and heavenly, as opposed to negative and earthly, height as opposed to depth, it is perhaps a reflection of the values of our essentially patriarchal society. Wholeness consists of the synthesis of these complementary forces, symbolised in alchemy by the important stage of the work known as the conjunction or marriage of the sun and moon.

The alchemical work, the long, mysterious and arduous process carried out by the alchemists in their laboratories, required the use of astrology, and alchemical texts are full of astrological and other forms of symbolism. The work itself may be seen as an essentially psychic or psychological process, its purpose being inner development rather than the production of tangible gold. C. G. Jung discovered to his amazement that the process described in the writings of the alchemists paralleled his own psychotherapeutic work, the images from his patients' dreams at crucial stages in therapy often echoing those found in the old texts. The reconciliation of the opposites within us, including our masculine and feminine sides, is as vital to what Jung called the "individuation process" as the sun-moon marriage of alchemy is to the achievement of its ultimate goal, the "philosopher's stone".

The sun and moon, then, are in astrology the most basic representation of masculine and feminine in the complex symbolic image of the individual that is the birth chart, and they stand for something more fundamental than the other planets. For this reason their functions on the birth chart are rather more generalised and difficult to grasp than those of the other planets, which are more narrowly and clearly defined.

In mythology, kings and heroes are often associated with the sun, and in an earlier age these heroic figures were subordinated to the goddess, who came to be associated with the moon, and were often identified both as her son and as her lover. The early kings, perceived as incarnations of the consort of the goddess, reigned for only a year or half a year, their power rising with the strength of the sun, and their end awaiting them in ritual murder, after which a new king would embody the solar principle. The sacrifice of the king was a symbolic enactment of the "death" of the sun, both in the withdrawal of its power in the winter and more dramatically in its daily descent below the horizon, when it appeared to sink into the underworld. This theme is met again in many myths of heroes who must undergo a "night journey", a descent into the darkness, before being spiritually reborn. From the story of the death and resurrection of Jesus it is possible to classify the founder of Christianity as a solar hero. In this case, as often, the masculine brightness is associated with the spiritual life, hence the tendency in the Christian tradition to view woman as somehow less spiritual, identified with the temptations of the flesh and carrying the projection of male sexuality.

The sun has to do with divine kingship, with centralised government (sun-worship was strong in Rome, as in Mexico and Peru, controlled by magnificent central powers), with brightness and splendour and the metal gold, with heroic fierceness, will-power and the fire of life.

The sun's sign, Leo, which rules the heart and backbone, is the sign of the king and of centrality. Those with an emphasis on this sign love to command and to occupy centre stage and enjoy the reassurance of an appreciative audience or adoring subjects. The cat, you may notice, has a preference for sitting in the middle of things, or where your attention is focused. Though generally sunny, generous and loyal, a sign with heart, Leonine demands for attention can amount to hysteria and impose considerable strain on those around them. This is also the sign of the child, playful and creative, yet insecure and hungry for love, a fiery and fixed sign.

The moon, on the other hand, as the light of the night, is associated with the enveloping, womb-like darkness out of which the sun emerges. She symbolises fertility and the woman's cycle. In the fiery sun's brightness, or broad daylight, everything is clear, but in the light of the watery moon there is mystery, ambiguity and uncertainty. Whereas the sun is more or less unchanging in appearance and shape, the moon is in constant rhythmic change, and rules the perpetual ebb and flow of the tides. In counterpoint to solar will-power she offers imagination and sensitivity. She is associated with silver and water.

The moon's sign, Cancer, is the sign of the mother or, as one astrologer has put it[15], of the mother/baby relationship. It is associated with feeding (it rules the breast which feeds and the stomach which receives food), and with the giving and taking of emotional nurturing and protectiveness which, when overdone, becomes smothering. Mother problems abound with Cancer. It is a deeply sensitive and imaginative sign, sometimes too much so for comfort, and inclined to take things personally. Its home-loving qualities and moodiness are often remarked upon, but less frequently mentioned and just as important are its imaginative/artistic tendencies. It is a watery and cardinal sign, associated with the sea and tides, and its symbol, the crab, can move sideways and approach things indirectly.

On the birth chart sun and moon represent two sides to our being, the sun having to do more with our conscious struggle to develop ourselves and make our way in life, the moon with that aspect of ourselves which we fall back into when not engaged in the struggle: the old, the natural, the comfortable, like a well-worn pair of slippers, our basic gut reaction. With the sun we push ahead; with the moon we simply respond instinctively, like a mother to the needs of her baby.

The sign the sun is in is the sign with which most of us identify. It is usually obvious, because to know it we need only to know the month of our birth. Curiously, this predominant interest in the sun sign corresponds to our cultural preference for the masculine. The moon sign is more obscure, we have to ferret it out of accurate tables. But despite the popularity of sun-sign astrology, the sun sign is not necessarily easy for us to live with. It has been noted that we often try to avoid rather than readily embrace those things represented by the sun's sign and house[16]. Whereas our sun sign speaks of the central life issues with which we must struggle, the moon sign suggests what makes us feel nurtured and at home.

There is a tendency, though it is not a universal rule, for women to live out the moon sign more, and men the sun sign, and for the other to be projected onto partners of the opposite sex.

A few words are necessary here on the important concept of projection. This is the mechanism by which we inevitably see in others those qualities, the desirable and especially the undesirable, which we are unaware of in ourselves, as is recognised in the aphorism that what we hate most in others is what is most detestable in ourselves. Older textbooks on astrology refer to the moon on a man's chart as representing the women in his life, but it may be argued that he will be drawn to the kind of women who represent his own undeveloped feminine side.

It is also said that the sun, according to its sign and contacts with other planets, tells us about the father of the native: for example, that his father is a violent person or a profoundly religious person. Similarly, the moon is held to describe the mother. Here again projection may come into the picture, as our parents or parent substitutes are the first carriers of our projections. In any case, there are of course inevitably resemblances between parent and child, so the sun on my chart can describe both my father and my own masculine side. In fact, particular signs and even degrees of signs tend to run in families.

In my own case, I found much to surprise me when I drew up my mother's horoscope — this was not the mother I knew from my perspective as daughter. On the other hand, she seemed very well-described by the moon on my own chart. Is this because I see my own lunar side in her? Is it that I came into the world with my own "mother image" already formed? Certainly my moon describes my experience of mothering. Different children of the same mother may have their moon in different signs. The mother is the same, but their experience of her different.

In the planetary order in current use, Mercury follows the sun and moon, but as Mercury occupies a unique position I shall return to him later and turn now to the next pair, Venus and Mars, whose astrological glyphs are used in science to represent the feminine and masculine genders.

VENUS AND MARS

Venus is associated with all that is soft and gentle, peaches and cream, beauty and harmony, art, decoration, pleasure. Venus or Aphrodite was the goddess of love and attraction, and was indolent, pleasure-seeking and rather vain. The planet is associated with copper, which is soft and pliable and used for making pleasing, decorative objects. The metal was named after the island of Cyprus, which was celebrated as Aphrodite's birthplace. Venus's placement on the birth chart relates to our capacity for pleasure and also to our ability to relate to others and draw them to us. Venus generally seeks to unite, as opposed to Mars who has a separative effect. She can be something of a dumb note on a man's chart, as men have a tendency to develop more strongly the thrusting power of Mars. Such men tend to leave the Venusian side of life to their womenfolk. The planet also relates to material goods, and is traditionally known as the Lesser Benefic.

Venus rules Taurus, the most pleasure-loving of all the signs, sensuous and appreciative of the good things of the earth, whether good food and wine, gardening and the land, quality goods, or, on a more sophisticated level, works of art. Taurus rules the throat and is often prominent on the charts of singers. It is a constructive sign, earthy and fixed, slow and patient, and often good at business. Its negative side is unadventurousness and resistance to change, and its predilection for appropriating what is pleasant and valuable for its own use, to the point of self-indulgence and possessiveness. Freud, whose sun was in Taurus, named one of his central concepts the Pleasure Principle.

In Libra, cardinal and airy, we see the other side of Venus, the principle of Eros or relationship. Opposite to Aries, an uncomplicated sign which goes straight for the goal, Libra is the sign in which self must be balanced against other, and partnership and harmony are greatly desired. She is mistress rather than mother. This is a relatively detached and unemotional sign, which places a great deal of store on seeing the other person's point of view. Those with Libra predominant in their charts can charm, or bend over backwards to placate, and have a reputation for finding decisions difficult. Curiously, though, Libra is not uncommon on the charts of military leaders, presumably because their ability to gauge the position and likely moves of their opponents makes them good strategists. Libra rules the kidneys, of which of course we have a pair, and which act to maintain the correct balance of water and other constituents in our bodies.

Mars is a fiery planet, traditionally associated with iron, which can be sharpened into knives and swords and which has a fiery colour in its natural state. He is hot and can be cutting. He is known traditionally as the Lesser Malefic, on account of his violent nature. Psychologically he is hero, warrior and lover, our capacity to dare, to assert ourselves and to take, and even fight, for what we want. He is the macho planet. Just as men are often out of touch with their Venus, leading to callousness, so women often have difficulty tapping their Mars and are prone to timidity, so that at the present time many women are drawn to assertiveness training to develop their Mars function rather than have their men live it out for them. In mythology Mars, known as Ares in Greek, was the god of war. He was considered to be the son of Hera, Zeus's wife, but conceived without the paternal assistance of Zeus. Thus he was identified as a product of the biological or feminine realm, and unrelated to the kind of spiritual masculinity associated with Zeus, who despised him.

Mars rules Aries, the first sign of the zodiac, fiery and cardinal. Aries, which in turn rules the head, befitting the headfirst rush of the battling ram, has a direct, full-ahead approach to life. It is a pioneering and competitive sign, full of energy to get things started and heedless of obstacles, though often rather bad at finishing things and careless of the feelings of others. The typical Aries is generally thought of as being rather physical and overtly fiery, but ardour and forcefulness can operate in a less obvious and more interior way.

Mars also rules the passionate sign of Scorpio, which is watery and fixed. It is a sign of immense strength, stamina and perseverance, a battling sign, yet at the same time secretive and subtle, hiding its depth and intense sensitivity. Its worst aspect is a propensity for paranoia and jealousy, but on the other hand it is second to none in its capacity to get to the bottom of things, and dig up what is hidden.

Scorpio rules the eliminative and reproductive organs, generally hidden from public view, and has a particular association with sexuality. It is sometimes symbolised by the eagle as well as the scorpion; the eagle is of course a bird of prey, and the symbol also suggests a potential for reaching heights as well as depths.

JUPITER AND SATURN

We have already associated the sun with kingship, but it was in fact Jupiter, or Zeus, who was king of the gods. After the sun and moon, Jupiter, known as the Greater Benefic, and Venus, the Lesser, are the brightest of the planets. To Jupiter belongs the principle of expansion. He rules things which are big and important, and foreign places. On the birth chart he represents the ability to go beyond the given situation, explore new possibilities, free ourselves from constraint. He is the planet of vision and optimism, and also of profligacy, that is, of giving, spending and wasting, as opposed to conserving. He is associated with the enquiring, philosophical mind and also with religion, faith, spirit. The worst of Jupiter is not his wastefulness, as is often said, but his sometimes dangerous refusal to acknowledge any limitations and his ability to carry us through enthusiasm into dogmatism and hypocrisy. Like the god, who was notorious for his infidelities, Jupiter is somewhat fickle and unstable. He has a reputation for good luck, which is partly due to the self-fulfilling tendency of positive expectation. The metal ruled by Jupiter is tin.

Jupiter rules Sagittarius, fiery and mutable, a sign with a careless love of freedom, generous, often fun-loving and generally good company, usually keen to acquire an understanding of a wide range of things. Its failing is the irresponsibility that goes with making promises under the influence of passing enthusiasm. It is a sign good at putting up a convincing front, and somewhat prone to over-optimism and over-indulgence. It rules the liver and also the thigh, those with an emphasis on the sign tending to enjoy walking and riding, and by extension travelling in general.

Jupiter's other sign is Pisces, the last sign in the zodiac. It is a chameleon-like sign, and those in whom it predominates often have a remarkable ability to change with their surroundings and company. As Pisces can easily feel its way into any role or mood it is a favourite sign among actors, dancers and musicians, but this can mean a problem with boundaries, uncertainty about one's own identity and a tendency to lose oneself in others. This is the most sensitive and unstable of all signs, being watery and mutable; it is prone to psychism and gifted with a delicate imagination. Drug and alcohol problems are not uncommon with Pisces, and it often has an unworldly orientation. Pisceans incline to the perspective from which all is perceived as one, and all positions are relative (Einstein, author of the theory of relativity, had the sun in Pisces). It can be a slippery and evasive sign, able to shift from one way of looking at things to another. It rules the feet.

Whereas Jupiter expands, Saturn, the Greater Malefic, contracts. He (although associated with the feminine earth element he is named after a male deity) rules limits and boundaries. Although we may prefer Jupiter's feeling of growth and optimism, nothing can be achieved without the concretising power of Saturn. A sense of heaviness belongs to him, and he rules the metal lead. He is the planet of structure, form and measurement, and of cold and rigidity. Psychologically he is associated with realism and matter-of-factness, with seriousness and responsibility, inhibition and reserve, and with material security and keeping things under control. As opposed to the elation that belongs to Jupiter, Saturn has a propensity for depression. Saturn's placement on the birth chart points to that area where we feel least confident and therefore most defensive, and to the qualities we feel we lack, and often work hard to develop.

The first sign ruled by Saturn is Capricorn, a cautious sign, down-to-earth and generally reliable, willing to take on responsibilities and good at organisation. It is reputedly ambitious, although this is not necessarily expressed in the obvious, worldly way, and means rather that those with this sign strong in their charts have an ability to set their minds on a goal and work steadily towards it; they are capable of making sacrifices and putting up with hardship along the way, and sometimes rather attached to the hair-shirted approach to life. It is perhaps an unglamorous sign, and at its worst is cold, calculating and stingy and rigid, but often stable, supportive and practical. It is cardinal and earthy, and rules the knees and the skeletal structure. Saturn's restrictive power is well reflected in the case of a man in whose chart Saturn and Capricorn were prominent and who was feeling a need for change. He found himself doodling pictures of a man surrounded by a square box, symbolising his sense of restriction. This is also the sign of the father, and father often looms large in the Capricornian psyche.

Saturn also rules Aquarius, another sign which is good at structure, but in a more abstract way. It is a sign particularly noted for its detachment and ability to handle things in an impersonal manner. It usually has high, humanitarian ideals but can have difficulty when it comes to more intimate matters such as personal relationships. Typically Aquarians have plenty of ideas about how society should be run, but are strong individualists and like to remain aloof from the group themselves. The sign has a rather paradoxical nature. Those with a strong Aquarian element can hold very obstinately to their views (it is a fixed and airy sign), but are prone to sudden changes and a kind of bloody-mindedness. While some Aquarians are more restrained and Saturnian in their conduct, many have a powerful rebellious streak and enjoy shocking. This may be attributed to the co-rulership of Uranus (see below). They often have ideas rather ahead of their time. Aquarius rules the calf and shin.

MERCURY

Mercury is the odd planet out in that he has no partner, and despite being named after a male god is both masculine and feminine. Mercury, or Hermes, is in fact generally depicted as youthful and unbearded, so as not to appear clearly male. His role as divine messenger has been discussed above (see page 69), as has his association with speech and communication and his talent for trickery. He rules the flow of information in and out, up and down, our capacity to learn and teach, and the to and fro of local transport and mobility. His metal, mercury or quicksilver, conveys the nervous energy and rapidity of the planet, and astronomically Mercury moves faster than any other planet except the moon. Mercury rules our capacity to name things and make distinctions between them, but also to make connections. He shares with Jupiter the rulership of the mutable signs, both planets having a rather elusive and tricky character, and being good at disguises. The spirit Mercurius is the central figure in alchemy, embodying all the forces of contradiction, both male and female, separator and binder, the highest and the lowest.

Gemini is the sign that most clearly expresses Mercury's mobility, and belongs to the air element. It is a light and often playful sign, with a liking to be on the move and a certain mischievousness. Somewhat detached, as are all the air signs, it enjoys talking about things, often preferring to observe rather than participate; strongly Geminian people make good communicators and link-people, good at bringing others together. They like variety and tend to find commitment irksome, which can be a problem for others. They can be tricky and evasive. It is of course the sign of the twins, and the Geminian tends to like having more than one option, more than one job, more than one partner, and this attraction to double situations can manifest itself in all aspects of life. A highly Geminian friend of mine lives in a double house with two front doors and has twin daughters.

In the myth of the twins Castor and Pollux, the two took turns at playing the roles of mortal and immortal, human and god, and the Geminian can be very up and down, now bright and snappy, now cynical and alienated. Gemini rules the arms and hands.

Fleet Mercury, with his winged sandals, also rules the earthy sign of Virgo, a sign concerned with usefulness. To Virgo belongs the capacity to create order by putting everything in its rightful place and separating the wheat from the chaff. The human body is one area where Virgo likes to bring order, through the role of healer, which is associated with this sign and with Mercury himself, one of whose attributes is the staff with two intertwined serpents, emblem of the medical profession. The connection between body and mind is an issue which often preoccupies Virgoans. Another area where they often excel is craftsmanship, and work which requires precision and attention to detail. The unlovely side of Virgo, often caricatured, is a certain obsessive-compulsive tendency, a preoccupation with order and cleanliness and a fear of chaos, a need to keep putting things straight, which can be very irritating. Because they are so sensitive to things which are not quite right, strongly Virgoan individuals can be critical of the failings of others. Virgo rules the intestines, where the process of sorting out the useful from the unwanted takes place.

THE EXTRA-SATURNIAN PLANETS

We have now covered all the signs, but are left with the three extra-Saturnian planets, discovered in modern times. There are still some astrologers who reject these planets, claiming that astrology was already complete without them; but, for the most part, they are considered important, and the majority of astrologers today consider them co-rulers of certain signs. There is further discussion of these planets and their discovery in Chapter 7. The three planets spend so long in each sign, and form aspects between themselves for such long periods, that their position on our chart must in many respects be considered as a generation factor rather than a personal one. For this reason they are considered to relate to collective rather than personal functions, and to be rather less under our personal control than those planets within the bounds of Saturn. They can be extremely powerful on the natal chart when they touch some more personal planet or point.

Uranus is the planet of shock, rebellion, revolution and individualism. He has a distant and impersonal quality, and tends to function in a sudden and unpredictable fashion. He is insistent on freedom, and autocratic in his behaviour. The Uranian individual may appear erratic and sometimes outrageous and often has highly original ideas and approaches to things, liking to be different and opposed to the prevailing orthodoxy. He is considered to co-rule Aquarius in uneasy partnership with Saturn, towards whose conservatism and sense of proper form he is extremely antagonistic. He appears to be an airy planet.

Neptune is a watery planet, and represents the principle of dissolution and merging. His orientation is distinctly unworldly, and one may praise his spirituality or condemn his escapism. Those with a strong Neptune often feel at odds with the world, having a sense that there is some better place devoid of the banality and abrasiveness of physical existence. They run the gamut from mysticism to drug-abuse, taking in idealism and art on the way. There is an extremely elusive and sometimes magical quality about this planet, and a disregard of definition and precision in favour of all that is subtle, ineffable and nebulous. He can enchant and confuse. Neptune is said to co-rule Pisces, for obvious reasons.

Pluto is usually considered to co-rule Scorpio, with which again he has obvious similarities. He is associated with the dark side of life, with death and violence and the struggle for survival, with the destructive capacity that lurks in all of us. He has to do with power in its most primitive sense, but also with the ability to penetrate mysteries and sense what is going on beneath the surface, and a strong Pluto is a great benefit to the psychotherapist, having a particular connection with depth psychology. Those with a strong Pluto can be ruthless and paranoid, as can Scorpios, but can also be unflinching in confronting the more unpleasant aspects of life.

Planets in Signs

I hope that by now readers will have some sense of the way in which the symbolism of the planets on the birth chart can be related to the dynamics of human experience and psychology, and of the symbolic connections between the planets and the signs they rule. Greater detail can be found in numerous textbooks, some of which are named in the booklist on page 156, as can more elaborate descriptions of other elements of interpretation.

As they travel around the zodiac, the planets can each be in any one of the signs, and their nature is modified accordingly, as if the planet wears the clothing and adopts the style of the sign it is visiting. Mars does not cease to be Mars because it is in Mercury's sign or Venus's, but it will operate in the style of that sign, with a greater or lesser degree of ease depending on the nature of the sign in question and its compatibility with the nature of Mars. If Mars is in Gemini it will operate in a Geminian way, via communication. It will be experienced, for example, as a sharpness or forcefulness of speech, because the individual's Mars operates in that way: he asserts himself verbally. If Mars is in Saturn's sign of Capricorn his fiery power will be expressed in a controlled, or cautious, or structured way. In his own sign of Aries he will function particularly strongly and characteristically, while in the opposite sign, Libra, Mars's straightforwardness and urgency are somewhat complicated by the Libran need to see things from more than one point of view, and to consider what others may think. It is as if the planet were a verb and the sign a modifying adverb: I attack, go out to get what I want (Mars) cautiously (in Capricorn) or subtly (in Pisces) or enthusiastically (in Sagittarius).

Each planet is traditionally held to operate in a particularly fortunate manner, to be *exalted*, in one particular sign, a different one from those it rules. In Mars's case this sign is Capricorn, whose Saturnian self-control channels Mars's feverish energy in a calculated and practical way, like a well-trained army. In the signs opposite those which it rules, and in which it is exalted, a planet is said to be *debilitated*, to operate with more of a struggle. For Mars these are the Venusian signs of Taurus and Libra, and Cancer, the sign of fluctuation, maternal concern, and the indirect, sideways gait of the crab. A list of these signs of dignity or debility can be found in the glossary on page 157.

The Nodes of the Moon

Besides the planets, certain points are also considered in interpretation, the most important of these being the *moon's nodes*. Otherwise known as the Head and Tail of the Dragon, they oppose each other on the chart and are the points of intersection between the planes of the sun and the moon. They move round the zodiac in the opposite direction to the planets, completing the cycle in about eighteen years. They have a bad reputation in traditional astrology, being the points where the sun and moon are found at eclipses. There are different approaches to their interpretation, but it is generally agreed that they have a "fated" feel to them.

Houses

In addition to being in a particular sign, each planet is also located in a particular *house,* the houses being defined by the rotating position of the earth within the zodiacal belt, that is to say, by the exact place and time of day of birth. The house position of a planet tells us in what department of human experience the planet's function will be particularly strongly felt. One American astrologer[17] has put it this way: the planets tell you *what*, the signs *how*, the houses *where*. The houses containing the sun and moon are particularly important.

The first house begins at the ascendant, where the zodiac crosses the eastern horizon, and from there the houses are counted round anti-clockwise to the twelfth, which finishes at the ascendant. There are a number of different systems for determining the *cusps* or boundaries between the houses, but the ascendant is always the cusp of the first house, and the descendant the cusp of the seventh, and in most systems the MC/IC axis forms the cusps of the tenth and fourth houses. A cusp is always defined by the house which *follows* it, in anti-clockwise direction (see Fig. 2, page 36). The intermediate cusps are found by various formulae and can be looked up in published tables of houses. Briefly, the meanings of the houses are as follows.

The first house, sometimes referred to in its entirety as the ascendant, is particularly important. Each house is coloured by the style of the sign on its cusp, and ruled by the planet which rules that sign, and the sign on the first house cusp, the ascending or rising sign, colours the whole chart and describes in a general way the individual's style. The three most important factors on the chart are the sun, moon and ascendant, and the rising sign is often the most easily recognisable, as if every factor on the chart has to pass through that filter. Whether we like it or not, whether we are conscious of it or not, we cannot help dancing to that particular tune. The ascendant has been likened to a lens interposed between us and our environment, so that we see the world through the particular distortions or colour of that lens, and the world perceives the same distortion or coloration in us.

Suppose I have Aries rising. I will look about me and see challenge and the call to action everywhere, and will go to meet it. Others will then see me as a challenging, dynamic or forceful individual. Any planets in the first house, and particularly any in conjunction with the ascendant, will also come into the picture, Venus, for example, lending softness and charm, or Saturn inhibition, reserve, shyness, which I may strive to overcome. The word "personality" is sometimes attached to this house, but I do not find the term particularly helpful, for if it means anything it must surely involve the whole chart. The sun, moon and ascendant, while being the most fundamental elements in the chart, are the most difficult to define precisely. The ascendant dictates our style of presenting ourselves, inescapably there in our presence; it is a more external factor than sun or moon.

The meanings of the twelve houses derive from the twelve signs, the first house corresponding to the sign of Aries. It is the house which asserts our presence in the world. It also appears to relate to the body, which in a sense is what stands between our inner identity and the environment. Although other factors such as the sun sign contribute to the appearance, the ascendant most often describes the physical characteristics, and each sign has its particular physical expression. (Please bear in mind that the descriptions given are based on Western European racial types and race must also be an important factor.) Those with Sagittarius rising, for example, tend to have the long jawline of this horsy sign. Elvis Presley had such a jaw, and in his case the characteristic long face, small nose and fleshy lips of his sun sign Capricorn feature as well. Libra rising tends to give a smooth, rounded quality to face and limbs, Virgo a more angular appearance, Cancer a moony face, Leo above-average height and an upright carriage, the fixed signs generally a squarish look, Capricorn boniness, Scorpio thick, lowering eagle eyebrows, Pisces slightly bulging eyes like a fish, and a receding chin. The part of the body ruled by the sign is often remarkable in some way. Taurus can endow a lovely neck and throat, Cancer well-formed breasts in women, Aquarius a well-turned calf, Gemini delicate hands.

The second house relates to property and resources, our attitude towards these and the way we handle them. It may say something about our earning capacity, although I must say that I have never found any means, traditional or modern, that can accurately answer the question "Will I get rich?" Suppose a man has Mars in the second house: this could mean that his competitiveness comes out in this area, that his earning power is experienced as a test of his masculinity. The sun here makes possessions and material resources a matter of central concern, which in some cases may lead to the accumulation of a lot of personal property but can, as in the case of Karl Marx, mean that the whole issue of property is questioned in a big way.

The third house concerns communications, learning, teaching, school. Saturn here might mean that a child would be slow in learning to speak, and feel inhibited or inadequate at school, and that she would have to work hard to pass exams, or at least feel she had to. The third house also has connotations of transport and short journeys.

The fourth house relates to the home, to the emotional experience of early life, often forgotten, to one's roots and ancestry and in particular to the father. This is rather odd, as the fourth sign, Cancer, is the sign of the mother and some astrologers see this as the mother's house; but the traditional interpretation of the fourth as the father, though apparently illogical, seems to me to hold good. Planets here will generally first be experienced as qualities belonging to the father, and certainly attach to our early memories of home. Pluto in the fourth may mean some violence—that the father was violent himself, or died or experienced violence when we were young, or that he brought us into contact with the seamy side of life, perhaps through incestuous feelings or through his oppressive behaviour. It often indicates that there is some deep scar relating to our original home; it represents something dark to which we do not want ever to return. Frequently the *country* of birth has been abandoned for such reasons. Tradition says this is the house of the beginning and end of life, implying that death itself is a going home.

The fifth house I would call the house of play. It concerns those activities we take part in for the love of them, or out of a need to express ourselves, rather than because we have to. It is sometimes referred to as the house of creativity, and this means not only artistic creativity but also our children, our flesh and blood creations. It is the house of the inner and outer child. Jupiter in this house tends to correspond to an abundance of creative energy and a fun-loving and somewhat exhibitionistic quality, it being, in my experience, a position common on actors' charts.

The sixth house concerns work, routine, the daily round, and the Virgoan area of health problems. It has to do with order, inner and outer. If we have unruly planets here, such as Neptune, Jupiter or Uranus, we will find routine difficult or irksome, and we may experience them as manifesting in our work situation or in our colleagues, that is to say, we may project our sixth house onto our working environment, as we may project our own creative potential onto our children (fifth house). A strongly tenanted sixth house often attracts people to the healing professions.

The seventh house, opposite the first, is the house of the "other" as opposed to the self. It is the house of partnership, relating to any other individual we find ourselves in a one-to-one relationship with, but particularly when there is some sort of contractual arrangement, such as a marriage or business partnership. Traditionally it is also the house of "open enemies", that is, of the antagonist. In relationship terms, it describes some of the things we look for in a partner, or those aspects of ourselves we tend to project onto partners. Uranus in the seventh seeks excitement in relationships and independence, space to move and be an individual within them. If one is not aware of this need for freedom of movement, the likelihood is that one is drawn to a very Uranian partner who acts out that need and may even leave abruptly. It is a placement which easily feels partnerships as claustrophobic.

The eighth house opposes the second, the house of personal possessions, and is described as representing what belongs to, is shared with, or comes to us from others; in other words, it relates to things which belong and yet do not belong to us, and is generally being activated in some way when there are property disputes, or when we gain as a result of a legacy or a lottery. As the house corresponding to Scorpio it is also the house of death, that is the death of those near to us, and eventually our own, though it is a rash astrologer who would try to judge when death will come. It also relates to sexuality and the emotional aspect of relationships, and rules things which are hidden, such as occult studies and the unconscious, so that those with planets here tend to feel pushed to look beneath the surface. The fourth, eighth and twelfth houses, which correspond to the water signs, all seem to connect both with the unconscious and with death.

The ninth house is the house of the journey, which means both the inner, spiritual journey and outer exploration as through foreign travel. It reflects our religious or philosophical inclinations, our way of seeking answers to the ultimate questions of life. The moon here would indicate someone who was very naturally drawn to these questions.

The tenth, whose cusp is the culminating point, the midheaven, represents that aspect of ourselves which we show to the public, what role we fill in the world, how we are seen in our professional capacity. If we have a profession, it should express the qualities of the sign on the cusp, as well as of any planets in the house, so that with Venus here we would expect perhaps an artistic role or one concerned with bringing people together, keeping the peace or providing beauty or pleasure. It is also the house of the mother, or as some would have it of the father—but mother's unlived ambitions are often the driving force behind a child's eventual career.

The eleventh is the house of friends, and particularly of groups, of the circles we move in and of organisations we belong to. It is also concerned with the larger group of society as a whole, and our views on how it should be run, that is, our political beliefs. Neptune here, for example, is usually rather idealistic about how groups should operate, and sensitive to the feelings that go on in them.

The twelfth house is, like Pisces, difficult to get hold of. It seems to reflect things which it is beyond our power to control and has a connection with experiences of confinement in institutions such as hospitals and prisons where the individual is powerless. Usually people who work in institutions of this kind have planets here—I have known several people with Pluto in the twelfth who worked in psychiatric hospitals. It often seems that we are simply channels of the forces represented by twelfth house planets, that we use them only on behalf of others or of some greater cause, and those with planets here, especially the moon, are often rather mediumistic.

Aspects

The planets, then, on the birth chart, represent dynamic forces which operate in us; their nature is expressed through the qualities of the signs in which they are located, and is experienced with particular force in the areas

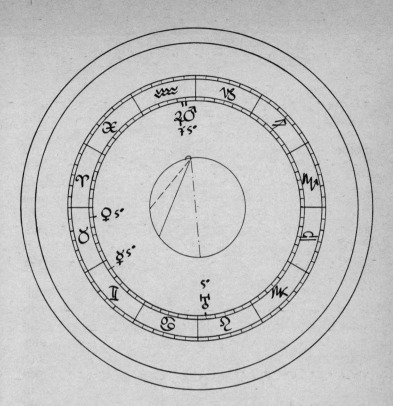

*Figure 5   Aspects. Mars, in Aquarius and at the top of the chart, is
in conjunction with Jupiter, in square to Venus in Taurus, in trine to
Mercury in Gemini and in opposition to Uranus in Leo. The lines in
the centre of the chart are drawn to help the eye pick out the aspects.*

indicated by their house positions. There is one last major
factor in interpretation and that is the way in which the
energy of two or more planets can be combined through
certain critical angles between them. We have already come
across the conjunction (see page 23), where two or more
planets are in the same degree, or within a few degrees of
each other, and the opposition, which speaks for itself. The
other major aspects are the square, or right-angle aspect, and

the trine, which spans a third of the circle. There are also a number of minor aspects. The trine is considered harmonious, the square and opposition conflictual, and the conjunction either, depending on the nature of the planets, but the precise kind of aspect is probably less important than the fact that there is one of these strong connections between two planets.

Suppose my Mars is in aspect with Saturn. When the fiery heat, the urgency and sharpness of Mars are engaged, the chill, inhibiting touch of Saturn is also experienced. Perhaps whenever I try to assert my presence, or take what I want, or compete, or prove my mettle, there will be some sort of experience of constraint. It may be that as a child I was made to feel guilty about my aggression, that my fiery urges were regularly thwarted or disapproved of. Somehow or other I cannot express my Mars freely. One man with a hard angle between these planets had a recurrent dream of a man with a severed arm, who would have been threatening and dangerous had he had the use of it. Mars/Saturn can mean that one's powers of assertion remain very inhibited, but it also often drives individuals, particularly men, who tend to identify with Mars more than women, to force themselves to overcome the constraint of Saturn. There is, in fact, a strong tendency among people with this combination to push themselves really hard and to overwork, as they strive constantly to overcome some inner obstacle.

The obstacle may be experienced as external, projected outwards, for it is inevitable that those aspects of ourselves that we repress are seen externally. I may experience myself as a dynamic, Marsy person always coming up against Saturnian authority figures whom I want to dynamite out of my way. The obstructive inner authority figure has not been acknowledged.

On the other hand, Saturn's defensive reserve feels attacked by Mars's impatient prodding. One Mars/Saturn woman often felt she was behind a wall, being attacked by missiles. If I identify more with the security and controlling power of Saturn, I may constantly feel my defences being bombarded by Marsy types who embody that side of me.

Or the whole combination of power and restraint may be experienced through another person. One woman with a Mars/Saturn conjunction in Cancer in the fourth house, the house of the father, described her potentially violent father, as she experienced him in childhood, as a dangerous Alsatian (Mars) on a leash (Saturn) held by her mother (Cancer).

When these two planets are in hard aspect on the birth chart the inner struggle between the two forces is habitual, and the task becomes to find a way for both to be expressed and befriended. Reconciling such different energies is easier when the planets are in trine aspect; in fact, they may not be experienced as conflicting at all, but as a naturally controlled forcefulness not unlike Mars's mode of operation in Capricorn, the sign of his exaltation. A working partnership between Mars and Saturn can obviously be highly effective and productive: it is power to act combined with realism.

Aspects form patterns on the chart, often shown by lines drawn between the planets, so that several planets may connect up into a formation. It may seem a little unfair that there are more difficult or hard aspects than there are easy or harmonious ones, but there is compensation in the fact that the hard aspects are more dynamic. Like the grit in the oyster shell around which the pearl is spun, they create a friction which obliges us to do something, to change. It is always pleasant to have a few trine aspects, in which the planets involved are experienced as blending nicely together, but they often seem to lack energy.

We have now covered the basic material of chart interpretation, although there are additional points and factors which can be used which need not concern us here.

The most important factors to consider are any emphasis on a particular sign, house or element; the signs of the sun, moon and ascendant and aspects to them, particularly solar aspects; and any planet which is emphasised by falling on or close to one of the four angles, particularly any planet rising (on the ascendant) or culminating (on the midheaven).

All these components build up a map of the individual life pattern, a map of the psyche. But the features on this map are symbols which, though they correspond to familiar landmarks of our experience, perpetually take on new forms.

Chapter 6

The Unfoldment of the Chart

Transits and Progressions

The birth horoscope is also a time map, and the chart factors which are particularly important at a given time can be determined from current *transits* and *progressions*. The principle of transits is easy to grasp. As the planets *in the sky*, in their continuing cycles, reach degrees of the zodiac circle which are particularly sensitive *on the birth chart*, such as where a natal planet or the ascendant is placed, there is a corresponding experience of the energy represented by the transiting planet in the individual's life. A transit from Neptune will reflect a Neptunian dimension entering our life, and it will enter through the gateway of the planet being transited. The experience of transits is one of the most direct ways in which we can get in touch with the planetary energies and learn about their qualities.

Suppose Neptune reaches the degree where Venus was at my birth. It is through my Venus, in the area of relationships, pleasures, or material goods, that I will experience the dissolving power of Neptune, and this will colour a period of a year or so, as Neptune moves very slowly, crossing and recrossing the same degree through retrogradation. The effect of such outer planet transits can, in fact, be experienced for a longer period than that, as the transit slowly builds up and eventually fades out.

This may indicate that I am ready for some kind of enchantment in relationships, a meeting with someone who has a magical, dissolving effect on me, so that I lose myself in that other person and see the world in soft focus. It could be experienced as a profoundly spiritual encounter, finding my soul-mate. It is likely to be a period involving some confusion or lack of clarity, and could even bring the dissolving of an existing relationship as my partner disappears into the mist. Most probably, my attitude towards relationships will be subtly modified during this period. If the more Taurean side of Venus is involved there may be a certain vagueness in my finances; perhaps I let money or possessions slip through my fingers because I am not really focused on material things. Neptune blurs boundaries. It could be a time when I positively swim in pleasure, and my sensitivity to what is beautiful is heightened, or my femininity is greatly enhanced. A Neptune transit of this kind can be an enthralling experience, but it also represents a time when I may be unrealistic, prone to wishful thinking and open to deception because I am living in a dream world. The planet that Neptune touches on my chart will indicate what facet of myself will be affected.

It is not only when Neptune is in the same degree of the zodiac as my Venus (that is, in conjunction with it) that I experience such developments, but also when Neptune aspects Venus by square, or some other kind of significant angle.

Saturn transits are times of enforced realism, when we are obliged to take responsibility for our actions and may reap what we have sown (for Saturn is the harvester god with his sickle or reaping hook). Developments are slowed down, we meet obstacles, but we can build firm foundations or consolidate to good effect. Uranus brings sudden change, times when we are pushed to shake ourselves out of a rut which we can suddenly bear no longer, and we often behave erratically, changing our plans repeatedly or making sudden and drastic decisions which may then be reversed by circumstances. Jupiter transits similarly tend to release energy; new options and visions open up, though sometimes mediated by none-too-pleasant experiences, and we are prone to enthusiasms and extravagant behaviour. With Pluto transits there is often the experience of violence on some level, perhaps a clash with forces, internal or external, beyond our control. We may have a sense of being imprisoned, with feelings of loss, frustration and anger, which can break out destructively. As with Saturn transits, these times can be depressing. They are not unlike the experience of death and mourning, an emptiness between what has been and what has not yet come into being. Sometimes the Pluto experience can be one of passionate emotional involvement, and as such be intensely pleasurable, but there is still the feeling of being overwhelmed, of having no choice. By the end of such a transit we usually feel we have entered a new phase of life.

Transits may manifest as external events, and this seems to be more true of those we experience in youth. But it is always helpful to relate the symbolism of events that "happen to us" to our inner reality. What does it mean if I have an accident or get sick? Is there a message in it, such as "You are speeding through life too fast and must stop and reconsider"? Under a Jupiter transit a woman met her future husband. He opened the door to her when she went to a friend's party. Now an opening door is both a beautiful image for Jupiter and a symbol of initiation into new possibilities, and indeed a door opened in her life. The outer so often reflects the inner, and a transit, like a double-sided mirror, reflects both. Incidentally, in the case just mentioned, the woman had in fact met the man several times before, but could not remember these meetings. The door was not yet ready to open.

While such developments may seem quite sudden, when we look at them in the context of our lives, we can see that the ground was being prepared long before. However, the transit itself marks some sort of crisis, which means literally a turning point.

Transits of the inner planets are fleeting and less far-reaching, but may still be noteworthy. Mars hits my Mercury and I am unusually sharp-tongued, or may burn my fingers, or find my car overheating. Again, it is useful to reflect on what this says about my current state of mind; my hastiness is surfacing; like my car, I am getting too heated.

As the planets orbit, they also move through the houses of the chart, and it is particularly noticeable when a slow-moving planet moves into a new house, bringing a change of emphasis. Here astrology offers a particular contribution to psychology, as the planets always travel through the houses in the same order. A time of stirrings of play and creativity, when Jupiter is in the fifth house, is invariably followed by a potential shaking or opening up in our working life, when Jupiter enters the sixth. When Saturn leaves the eighth house, often though not invariably a period of conflict, sometimes involving the break-up of a relationship or an experience of death, he enters the ninth and we strive to find meaning behind the suffering, in the consolation of philosophy or religion.

Alongside transits there are various systems of *progression*. The astrologer finds a new position for each of the chart's planets by moving them slowly on along the zodiac as the life progresses. The precise distance each planet is moved depends on the system employed. The new positions are then, like transits, compared to the natal positions, although unlike transits, the progressed positions do not correspond to actual planetary positions in the sky at the time of life in question. Any change of sign or house involved and any aspect formed between a progressed and natal planet is interpreted.

The manner of determining progressed positions may seem obscure or even arbitrary to the non-astrologer, yet progressions work. The most common system derives from the principle that each *day* of early life symbolises a *year* of later life, and astonishingly this proves meaningful in practice. The positions of the planets one day after the birth are taken to represent developments at the age of one year, positions two days after birth correspond to the age of two, and so forth.

By *secondary* progression, as this system is called, the outer planets move little, but the sun moves roughly one degree a year, corresponding to the amount it moves along the zodiac in one day. This means that by the time we are thirty, the sun's progressed position is thirty degrees from its natal position, having moved through a whole sign. At some point it may form a progressed aspect to Mercury, and this might imply an outstanding time for learning or teaching or writing. In practice, it is mainly progressions formed by the fast-moving planets that are considered, while the outer planets form the most significant transits.

Through transits and progressions the symbolism of the natal chart comes to life. We experience the different facets of our nature unfolding in the course of time. Understanding the nature of the time can be of vital importance; it means knowing what opportunities are at hand, and where our efforts are likely to be blocked. Even in a situation which is both painful and beyond our control, looking at the symbolic aspect of what is happening can give a new perspective and, by opening us up to the *meaning* of the experience, make it easier to bear. The principle of transit also reminds us that life involves constant change, and even the darkest transitions do not last for ever.

The Astrological Life Cycle

Behind the idiosyncratic pattern of the individual life path lies the generic development of our common humanity, a progress from birth through childhood and adulthood to old age, supposing we live long enough, with death as the inevitable final scene. Transitions from one phase of life to the next are still often marked by rites of passage, as they are in tribal communities: a party when the age of majority or retirement is reached, a *bar mitzvah* or confirmation ceremony, and very often promotion to a new kind of school at the onset of adolescence. The purpose of such rituals is the same as it has always been: to mark the acquisition of a new status and to affirm that it is time to leave behind what belonged to the previous phase.

Parents of small children note with pleasure, and often record, the date of the first step, the first word, the first accomplishment of a new task, and measure their own child's progress against that of other children, or of themselves at a similar age. Some children are said to be "precocious", or "advanced for their age", while some are "slow developers", all implying a developmental norm.

Each stage of life has its particular tasks and confronts us with new challenges, and a great deal of work has been done by psychologists and psychotherapists on the study of the early years of life, when the child is learning extremely fast and acquiring habits on which later development must be built. Not only must such tasks as walking, talking, using the hands and going to the potty be learned, but also, from the first months, emotional responses and the bases of social interaction. Where a task is not learned at the appropriate stage the opportunity may come around later, but where things have gone badly wrong, something may be irretrievably lost. For example, speech must be learned during a critical period of years, and a child deprived of human contact and the opportunity to learn to speak throughout this period will never fully accomplish this task. More recently the attention of psychology has shifted to later stages of development, such as the achievement of adult responsibilities, the mid-life crisis, the onset of old age.

The stages we pass through have been variously enumerated over the ages. The Pythagoreans with their predilection for the number four compared life's development with the four seasons of the temperate zone, an analogy still in common parlance ("the autumn of life", and so forth). Or we may prefer the division into three, corresponding to the three faces of the lunar goddess: maid, mother and crone, analogous to the waxing, full and waning moon. Jung has a simple, two-part division, the first and second halves of life. Our allotted span has also been divided into five, six, seven and eight stages, the "seven ages" approach, exemplified by Jacques' speech in *As You Like It* (Act 2, Scene 7), being the one most readily associated with astrology. Seven ages, of course, correspond to the seven traditional planets, although, on close examination, Shakespeare's seven scenes, while obviously based on astrology, do not fit exactly.

Astrology has its own statement to make about the developmental process, for in addition to transits of, say, Saturn or Neptune to an individual's sun, each transiting planet sooner or later completes its cycle and returns to *its original place* on the chart, on the way running through the whole range of aspects to that birth position. Naturally there is some degree of variation between individual charts, as planets do not proceed around the zodiac at a constant rate, all except the sun and moon going retrograde from time to time; but these continuing cycles are *approximately* the same for all. If we are lucky, we may live to see what is known as the Uranus return at the age of about eighty-four, when Uranus completes his orbit, or the third return of Saturn a little later, and in the interval since birth we will have passed through a pattern of overlapping, shorter cycles of the planets closer to the sun. The same process operates with progressions, except that only the moon ever makes a complete cycle by secondary progression during a human lifetime.

On account of the discovery of the slow-moving outer planets, which can form transits that colour relatively long periods, modern astrologers have placed greater emphasis on transits than earlier generations did. Of the outer planets, Saturn takes on average about 29½ years to return to its natal position, Uranus 84 years, Neptune 165 and Pluto 248 years. The transiting squares and oppositions, and to a lesser extent other aspects, of these planets also correspond to critical times, as the clock of these transit cycles inescapably measures out our shrinking potential lifespan.

Whether we are considering the conjunction or some other kind of aspect, there is a great emphasis at such times on the natal status of the planet in question, its house position, its sign, its natal aspects. At no other time are we likely to experience in a purer form the full meaning to us of the planet and its placement on the birth horoscope than when it is receiving a transit from itself.

Although much has been written about the first Saturn return at the age of twenty-nine to thirty, and about the Uranus opposition and Neptune and Pluto squares which occur in the middle years of life—and these will be discussed later in the chapter—little attention is usually paid to the returns of the inner planets, except for those of the sun. Earlier in this chapter (page 102) we saw that transits of, say, Mercury and Venus, though not without significance, correspond to quite minor changes, and when we consider that these planets return every year or so, and that the moon returns every month, we scarcely expect that these transits will be of major life importance. In the course of our life we may see a thousand lunar returns.

Think, though, of a tiny infant, for whom everything is new. After a hundred moons we can afford to be blasé, but to the impressionable babe, learning with a rapidity impossible in later years the fundamental lessons of life on which all later development will be based, that first lunar cycle, the first month of life, must be full of novelty and intensity. The experiences of the first two years of life are crucial to our well-being or lack of it in later years. Every psychotherapist knows how hard it is to repair damage inflicted at this tender age. The word "damage" is not meant to imply wanton cruelty by parents or minders, although this of course also occurs, but mistakes resulting from the ignorance of those responsible for the baby's welfare, and unavoidable accidents and misfortunes which affect the child's environment. The death or illness of the mother or mother-substitute at a crucial stage, the effects of material or emotional problems on the mother, hospital-isation of the infant itself, all these things can inflict lasting wounds on a helpless child who is still learning basic trust.

There exist numerous psychological models of early development, but they tend not greatly to contradict each other, and it is fascinating how well the model implicit in astrology fits those based on empirical research and the evidence of the therapist's consulting-room.

The moon on the birth chart connects with, among other things, our experience of mothering and being nurtured. Despite the feminist movement, the role of the mother is still often looked down upon not only by men, but by many women themselves, eager to enjoy the privileges earlier enjoyed by men alone. The irony is that the enormous power of the mother is not appreciated, the truth of the saying that "the hand that rocks the cradle rules the world". At the time when we are most malleable and most active in learning, when the basic emotional patterns that determine many of our later attitudes are set, it is the mother or mother-substitute who consciously or unconsciously moulds us. Her callousness can cripple us psychologically for life, her expectations are built into us, her ability to relate to us and meet our needs dictates our future ability to relate and to trust.

The moon's sign, Cancer, rules the stomach, and in the first few months of existence feeding is of central importance. If the food comes when it is needed, and the experience of feeding is unhurried and accompanied by feelings of loving intimacy, the expectation that needs will be met stays with the child in later life, providing a basic emotional security. If the infant is left hungry and screaming for long periods, or the mother has difficulty in feeding it, or is frequently agitated or impatient with her child, an early habit of anxiety develops which again runs as a thread throughout life. Many eating disorders as well as insecurities have their origin in these early days. Very few people can actually recall the experiences of this period of life, but they live on in us as emotional habits, the more powerful for being unconscious.

Our degree of emotional security, our ability to feel nurtured, our basic gut-level response to situations, tend to be indicated on the birth chart by the lunar aspects. Harsh aspects from Saturn suggest a coldness or depression in that early environment that continues to accompany us, Mars aspects hurry, agitation, abruptness, Uranus aspects unpredictability accompanied by anxiety, Pluto aspects oppression, smothering attention, anger or even violence.

The first transits to bring focus on these natal aspects are those formed by the moon during the first month of life, and the first squares, oppositions and conjunctions of the moon to the natal configuration are often accompanied by problems in the mother/child relationship. For example, the mother of a baby with a moon/Pluto conjunction developed a lactating problem exactly as the first lunar square came in. In her anxiety and guilt she tried desperately to meet the baby's needs, and we can but imagine how this was experienced by the child — possibly as an overwhelming and unwelcome emphasis on the feeding process. The seven-day-old certainly cried bitterly. One can imagine that at each critical transit to the basic natal configuration some slight difficulty might rub in the pattern a little more.

Other transits may occur during these first tender

months, to complicate matters. The maternal grandmother of a baby with a moon/Saturn opposition died when the child was just over two weeks old. The opposition was a little over one degree from exact at birth, and at the time of the death Saturn had travelled that one degree and was now *exactly* opposite the moon. In response to this event the mother, already overburdened for a variety of reasons, was naturally absorbed in her own grief, so that the child could not get the warm response she looked for. Her early months were lived in an atmosphere of mourning and desolation, and she was later to be subject to frequent bouts of depression.

It is generally supposed that during the first months of life the baby, which before birth was completely contained by and inseparable from the mother, has still no sense of being a separate individual. A mother with a tiny infant often intuitively knows what the baby needs, even if it is in another room, as if it were still part of her. As far as the child is concerned, there are pleasant and unpleasant experiences, but it has no sense of self and other, of inner and outer. These distinctions develop gradually with consciousness.

Beyond the phase of intense lunar preoccupation comes a focus on the cycles of the sun, Mercury and Venus, all bunched together. With the emerging sense of a separate identity and the capacity for creative play (the sun) comes a need to relate to others (Venus), to the mother as a separate person, to try to please her and to communicate with her (Mercury). As the monthly lunar cycles begin to become routine, so the emphasis shifts to the annual and near-annual cycles of these next three planets, and their phases. Mercury may possibly relate to walking as well as speech, but perhaps here the first semi-sextile or thirty-degree aspect of Jupiter to its natal position might be considered. Jupiter's cycle is nearly twelve years, and consequently he spends on average a year in each sign, so that this first aspect falls at an average age of twelve months.

It should be emphasised that I am not claiming that the first Mercury return, which occurs somewhere between eleven and thirteen months, is going to correspond to the first word, or the first Jupiter semi-sextile to the first step, in a mechanical fashion. Obviously, there is great variability in these developments from one child to the next. But the overlapping of these planetary cycles does symbolise nicely the normal developmental phases, which also overlap. For astrological correlations to the stages which mark an *individual* child's development we must look to other kinds of transits, and we must also consider whether the natal aspects in themselves have anything to say. A child started walking at nine months, when the moon's north node came into conjunction with Jupiter, and another first walked at ten months, when Mars crossed his ascendant in Sagittarius. Both these early walkers had an emphasis on the sign of Sagittarius, which rules the thigh and walking. Mars transits in early life often seem to coincide with the sudden achievement of a new task, and particularly when this takes place earlier than expected.

Incidentally, the solar return, which comes round every year on or near our birthday, has long been accorded a particular significance by astrologers. Each year it reaffirms who we are, what we are in the process of becoming. A chart is drawn up for the moment the sun reaches its exact natal degree and minute, and for the place where the person is living at the time, and is used as a tool for forecasting major developments during the following year. The houses of the sun and moon on this chart tend to stand out as being of particular relevance.

By the time of the first Mars return at the age of about two years we are at the tantrum stage, trying out our power to get what we want, beginning to separate from mother and learning autonomy. The potty (associated with the eliminatory sign of Scorpio, traditionally ruled by Mars) is often the focus of a battle of wills, as the child learns control of the sphincter muscles. The lesson of this phase is sometimes referred to as "self-mastery".

During this period it is important that the child's new powers of assertion find firmly defined parental boundaries to kick against, otherwise it will feel insecure. Boundaries and discipline are symbolised by Saturn, and the first Saturn semi-sextile falls, on average, at the age of about two and a half years. As we have already seen, Saturn also symbolises the father, and discipline is usually considered to belong to the father-role, as it is difficult for the person doing the mothering to be sufficiently detached from the child. As we begin to make acquaintance with the outside world, Jupiter comes more into play, but the capacity for abstraction and speculative thought does not really develop much before the first Jupiter return at the age of eleven or twelve, which is also the age when all the possibilities of adult life really begin to open up, and there is frequently a growth-spurt at this time.

Saturn is the planet of responsibility, and also of inhibition and self-consciousness. His first square falls around the age of seven, when the first teeth (teeth are ruled by Saturn) are falling out, often producing feelings of extreme shyness. The opposition at fourteen to fifteen years tends to coincide with the peak of self-consciousness and teenage awkwardness. The next Saturn square coincides roughly with the first Uranus square (twenty-one to twenty-two). Here, symbolically, is a conflict between the urge to express individuality (Uranus) and the desire to be seen as a responsible adult (Saturn).

The crisis of the first Saturn return is a very well-known one among astrologers, and a favourite time for people to seek a chart reading. Like all Saturn transits, this is a time for realism, a time when material security tends to be important and responsibilities are shouldered, willingly or unwillingly. If early adulthood has been a period of steady progress and wise decisions this can be a time when efforts are rewarded and increased responsibility goes with improving status.

All too often, however, the choices we make in our late teens and twenties are still over-influenced by parental expectations, or else result from a naive rebellion against them. As the Saturn return approaches we cannot escape the reality of any disjunction between our chosen direction and our own true needs and abilities. It is common to make career changes around this time, and early marriages often fail here, as a new sense of accepting responsibility for one's own life sets in. The age of thirty is a milestone after which society finds it less easy to accept those "follies" associated with youth. Now middle life approaches and one is an adult in earnest.

The house in which Saturn is placed on the natal chart is usually of considerable importance at this time, its affairs demanding commitment and hard work, and there are likely to be distinct developments in this direction from the time when Saturn enters his own house. When he is natally in the ninth house of spiritual quest, for example, the authority of a religious establishment is usually something to be grappled with at some point, and the issue is likely to come up at the Saturn return. This may mean commitment to a particular spiritual authority or even the establishment of one's own authority in a religious or philosophical context, or a period of struggling to give form to one's theories or beliefs.

The next major astrological markers in the human life-cycle are those which colour the mid-life period. A mid-life crisis is not something which happens at a clearly-defined point, and need not coincide with the Uranus opposition or Neptune and Pluto square, but these are important times, nevertheless, and the natal and transiting house positions of the planets tend to be in focus. As the length of our past life grows to match our remaining life expectancy a prolonged period of adjustment sets in. The principles we lived by in youth no longer feel appropriate to our years. As children grow up and leave home the tasks of parenthood are left behind and we are left facing new possibilities and challenges, and have to find new goals.

The Uranus opposition arrives in the late thirties or early forties, and can best be described as an impulse to break out in some way and do something we have not tried before. As under other Uranus transits, we are inclined to be erratic and unpredictable, and to keep changing our plans, or finding that circumstances seem to keep changing. People often make sudden decisions to get married, get divorced, emigrate or something equally drastic, only to change their minds again just as suddenly. They are looking for some radical change, but they are not sure what it is. It is a period of shake-up, a time when long-hidden needs and desires awaken, unexploited resources cry to be let out of the closet and familiar patterns feel restrictive or boring. It can often feel like a chance for a last fling.

The Neptune square is inevitably more subtle, and is also more variable in the time of its occurrence, because of the longer and less regular cycle of the planet. There may be experiences of loss, and of the gradual slipping away of things that have been important, such as family duties, and there can be bewilderment and uncertainty. There may also be a questioning of earlier values, and a new kind of inwardness, a sensitivity to things which had hitherto escaped our notice. As a general rule (and there are always exceptions to such rules), the second half of life involves a decrease in concern about external and material matters and an increase in the importance given to inner life and spiritual values.

With the Pluto square, which can fall as early as the early forties or as late as sixty-five, depending on the year of birth, the issue of mortality generally has to be confronted.

There may be deaths close to us, or some illness or other development which obliges us to face the issue. We may also be confronted with our own destructiveness as never before, or with the darker aspects of our nature which cast a shadow over the image of ourselves we like to see. Issues of power and powerlessness feature, and anger and frustration at the ageing process and at what cannot be changed. We are forced to shed some of our attachments or illusions, and that letting go can lead to a healing and renewal.

So far I have scarcely mentioned progressions. The system of secondary progressions operates on the basis that positions on the second day after birth correspond to the second year of life, those on the third day to the third year, and so forth. This means that those very early *transits* of inner planets which make their impression on the baby in its first few months come up again as progressions later in life. Put another way, the pattern of transits in those first three months translates into an identical pattern on a much greater scale, covering our entire life, in the progression system. Some astrologers also use additional sets of progressions corresponding to a day for a month and a day for a week, so that the same pattern operates simultaneously on several different timescales.

I have not studied a great deal of data on the astrology of early development, but it has several times struck me that there seems to be a connection between what was happening at the time of the original transit and what happened at the time of the subsequent progression. A child whose mother had a feeding problem when the child was two weeks old became anorexic at around fourteen years, and one who was sent to live with relatives at a similar tender age, on account of the break-up of the parental marriage, suffered a breakdown at the time of the progression. I do not wish to imply some sort of mechanical process at work, but it is a fact that such early occurrences do have later effects, and the symbolism of astrology is a means of drawing our attention to such links.

In psychotherapy it is generally recognised that life brings round again opportunities to work through developmental stages that were left uncompleted. An individual who was blocked by circumstances from going through the normal phase of teenage rebellion and boy-meets-girl scenarios can go through a "teenage" phase in the thirties or forties, and the child who was forced to do things on his own too early can in later life go through a period of dependency, on an understanding partner perhaps, or on a therapist, and emerge with a new-found independence. With the language of astrology at our disposal we can often see such opportunities coming, signified by transits or progressions.

All this talk of the stages of life, each one bringing us successively nearer to the inevitable end, and of opportunities to repair earlier damage, may be felt as somewhat gloomy, but to me there is also something quite inspiring in this image of overlapping cycles. Those earliest cycles, such as that of our first moon, are very small, and our perceptions at that level of development very narrow. The process of growth and development carries us out in ever wider circles of expanding experience and con-sciousness, an essentially Jupiterian process, while the smaller cycles are still there and accessible in the centre of our being.

Chapter 7

New Planets

The passage from astrology as practised during the Renaissance, when it was deeply embedded in our culture, to the astrology of the modern era, was marked by the shift to a solar-centred astronomy and by the discovery that there were planets beyond the orbit of Saturn. According to the Ptolemaic model of the universe, which was accepted until the sixteenth century when Copernicus published his daring theory that the earth travelled around the sun, the sphere of Saturn encompassed those of all the other planets. In fact, Copernicus' idea was not a new one. Such a theory had been known in the ancient world, propounded by Aristarchos of Samos in the third century BC. But Ptolemy's earth-centred universe had become so built-in to Western consciousness and religious doctrine that it was an enormous shock to find the earth demoted to the status of a satellite.

Given a more accurate picture of the solar system and the development of the telescope, it was but a matter of time before the new planets, invisible to the naked eye, were observed. By the time Uranus was discovered in 1781 astrology was in decline, and this event sent further shock-waves through the body of astrological knowledge. Saturn had been the outer wall of the planetary system, and now it was shattered. The earth had shrunk in importance and now space was expanding. Where did this new body belong in the astrological system so long accepted as complete in itself, with its seven planets governing the twelve signs in a symmetrical pattern of rulerships?

Symbolically, it is highly appropriate that the planet whose discovery was responsible for shaking up the old system, and coincided with a time when the old order, as symbolised by conservative Saturn, was being challenged on many fronts, should have been the one now understood as the bringer of shock and sudden, radical change. What is more, the symbolism of Uranus as it has subsequently emerged reflects astonishingly the age in which the planet was discovered.

It was the age, as has been remarked earlier in this book, when science as we now understand it came into being, and Uranus has a quality of detachment and radical enquiry that well suits this new trend. Moreover, the period of Uranus' discovery saw the emergence of a new kind of politics, as exemplified in the aspirations of the French revolution to liberty, equality and fraternity, distinctly Uranian principles. In fact, the planet of revolutionary change and the freedom of the individual was discovered between the American war of independence and the French revolution. Then again, the discovery of Uranus in 1781 was followed a decade later by the publication of Galvani's research into electric current, which also connects with the planet's shock function. In my experience, problems with electrical and electronic equipment almost invariably coincide with transits to my Uranus, and this is a widely recognised phenomenon. The name Uranus gradually came to be favoured over two other contenders, and the television aerial glyph is based on the initial of the planet's discoverer. Herschel, after whom it was suggested the planet should be named. The second name suggested was Sidus Georgicus, after the reigning monarch. The mythological name was derived from the existing series: Saturn was father of Jupiter, Uranus father of Saturn. Uranus is the remote sky god, whose potency fearful Kronos/Saturn destroys.

In 1846 another planet was discovered, and given the

name of Neptune. Appropriately enough, there was considerable confusion over the question of who was responsible for the discovery of the planet, as two scientists independently had predicted its location on the basis of perturbations in the orbit of Uranus. Once again it is relevant to compare the meaning attributed to the planet with contemporary developments. Two years after its discovery there was a wave of uprisings throughout Europe, and while Neptune is not considered revolutionary in the manner of Uranus, it is often felt to rule socialism, on the grounds that this is an idealistic, Utopian movement. Socialist theory was developing apace in the 1840s, and in 1848 the Communist Manifesto was published. On the scientific front, 1846 saw the first use of ether anaesthesia for surgery, and Neptune is distinctly associated with both gas and sleep. 1850 was the year of the first submarine. There was also a wave of interest in psychism, another Neptunian phenomenon, around this time, the first manifestation of which was the claim by the Fox sisters of New York State that they had received communications from disembodied spirits by means of knocking. After this, many people in America and Europe discovered medium-istic powers, eventually organising themselves into groups, and somewhat later, scientists began to research these Neptunian phenomena.

Neptune in myth was originally a god of earthquakes, and as earthquakes brought tidal waves to the marine world of Greece, he came to be a sea god. I would associate the planet not with Neptune alone, but with various ancient sea gods such as Nereus and Proteus, the latter known for his elusive nature and ability endlessly to change shape. The glyph for the planet is the god Neptune's trident, which is similar to the Greek Letter *psi*, used for psychic phenomena. In line with its astrological meaning, the planet's surface is permanently covered by clouds.

Pluto was discovered in 1930, at a time when totalitarian

regimes were spreading, and two years before the first man-made nuclear reaction inaugurated a new and terrifying age. Pluto is associated with the crude exercise of power in general, and appears to have a particular connection with atomic power and plutonium. The god, known as Hades in Greece, was the terrible god of the underworld, lord of the dead, and the planet astrologically symbolises underground activity in all senses, from tunnels through spying to the unconscious, and is also associated with death and annihilation. The naming of this planet is a fascinating example of the mysterious process by which astrologically appropriate names are allotted by those with anything but astrology in mind, as if the name itself is just waiting to be discovered. There were those who wished to name the new planet after Percival Lowell, who had predicted the discovery of a planet outside the orbit of Neptune, but others were in favour of a name from classical mythology, in line with those of other planets. Suggestions poured in to the Lowell Observatory in Arizona, and it was in fact an eleven-year-old girl from Oxford, England, who first proposed the name of Pluto. Rumour has it that her inspiration was the Walt Disney cartoon dog rather than the god. One of the reasons the name was favoured was that the opening letters were Percival Lowell's initials, and they still form the basis of one of the glyphs for the planet (P). A further entertaining detail is that one of the objections raised to this name was a possible association with a popular laxative of the time, known as Pluto Water. Pluto, allotted to co-rulership of Scorpio, is associated with elimination and the eliminative organs of the body.

The resurgence of astrology in the twentieth century came largely out of the work of that nineteenth-century Neptunian phenomenon, the Theosophical Society. This organisation was founded in 1875 by Mme Blavatsky, to promote the spiritual development of its members and of humanity, through the study and practice of certain esoteric teachings. By the second half of the twentieth century, when astrology began to find a new popularity, the three new planets had been fairly well absorbed into the system, although this did involve disrupting the old, symmetrical pattern of sign rulerships. More recently, a new heavenly body has sent ripples through the astrological community, and is pushing for recognition. Whether it will be fully incorporated into the astrological pantheon remains to be seen, but there are an increasing number of astrologers, including myself, who feel that it is an object of importance. This "planetoid", discovered by American astronomer Charles Kowal in 1977, was given by him the name of Chiron, apparently because of its proximity to Saturn, in myth the father of Chiron. In fact, although Chiron's orbit lies for the most part between those of Saturn and Uranus, it is extremely irregular and passes outside the orbit of Uranus.

I should emphasise that at the time of writing it is less than a decade since the discovery of Chiron, and we are still at the stage of groping to understand his significance. What I have to say on the subject concerns observations confined to a specific theme, and if Chiron has the status of a planet we should expect a whole complex of related meanings. The following pages detail some ideas and findings which mainly concern a very specific area of Chiron's activity, but one that I feel is probably crucial to understanding his role.

In approaching the possible meaning of a new heavenly body, we are given two interconnected clues, if we are to judge from the cases of Uranus, Neptune and Pluto. These are the name the planet is given and contemporary developments. What aspects of the mythological figure after whom the planetoid was named will eventually prove relevant to the story, time will tell, but the myth is interesting in its own right, and of particular relevance to those astrologers who see themselves as healers in some sense. Chiron is a most peculiar figure in Greek mythology, whose part-animal form suggests great antiquity. Although some of the gods of the classical pantheon can change their shape, they are normally imagined in human form. Chiron is half-man, half-horse, in other words a centaur; yet he is to be distinguished from the other centaurs, notorious for their rowdy behaviour and penchant for drinking large quantities of wine, because he is born of completely different parents. He is unique, in a class of his own. One of the keywords suggested for his astrological counterpart is "maverick", and this the myth appears to back. According to the version handed down from classical times, Chiron is the son of Kronos and the nymph Philyra (Lime Tree). To escape Kronos' attentions Philyra turns herself into a mare, but Kronos rapes her in the form of a horse. The result of this union is Chiron, and so distressed is Philyra at his appearance that she begs Zeus, who has somehow anachronistically got into the story, to turn her into a lime tree.

Now Chiron is a teacher, which I suspect is also an important factor in interpreting the astrological Chiron, and it is especially young future heroes who gravitate to him for instruction: Achilles, Jason, Perseus, Herakles, the twins Castor and Pollux and more besides. They come to him in his cave, for their teacher does not live in a house but in a primitive earth-dwelling, as befits the animal side of his nature.

Chiron's school does not provide a particularly academic education. His name means in Greek "hand-being", handyman, manual worker, craftsman — he's clever with his hands, and he teaches useful skills. Ultimately, you could say the two principal subjects taught are killing and healing. He teaches his boys riding, gymnastics, hunting, making and using weapons: that is, he trains them in the arts of warfare, and in this context he also teaches them how to patch up wounds. Healing, here, is one of the skills of war. This is where Chiron differs from any other martial arts teachers who might be around: he teaches these important additional healing skills. His methods are the internal and external application of herbs and the use of the knife in surgery. He himself appears to have some more arcane healing powers: for example, he makes a blind man see.

In addition, he teaches divination and prophecy, which again are very useful. (Astrology is mentioned, but this must be a late addition to the myth, for, as we have seen, astrology was a late import to Greece.) Ethics is included in the curriculum to put the rest in context – Chiron may not be an intellectual, but he's not uncivilised – and so is music. In fact, it appears that music forms part of his *materia medica* too, for Pindar talks of his using "soothing incantations" in his healing. Music has long been considered psychologically healing.

Basically, Chiron teaches the art of surviving in a hostile world, tempered by philosophy and music. It is an education for heroes. But one of his pupils is Asklepios, known as the "father of medicine", and it is perhaps as Asklepios' teacher that Chiron is best-known.

In the *Iliad*, the great Homeric poem which describes the Trojan war, there are numerous accounts of people being wounded and treated, and the pupils of Chiron are often called upon to administer remedies. This draws our attention to the connection between killing and healing, the fact that there is no better place to practise and study medicine than the battlefield. Both in ancient and in modern times surgery has been developed in the context of war; the physician needs an intimate knowledge of wounds and sickness. For many people today the most unacceptable face of medicine is the millions of sentient beings who are tormented to death for the sake of our health, and of course human patients are also to some extent experimented on and may get sick or even die from their medicines. According to one account, human sacrifices were offered to Chiron in Thessaly, and we still seem to need to make blood sacrifices to the god of healing.

It is, therefore, no accident that the healer is also a killer. The oracle of Apollo (Apollo shares with Chiron the themes of healing, slaying with the arrow, and music) tells Telephos, who has been wounded by Achilles, that "the wounder heals", and so Telephos seeks out his enemy and is made whole with the rust from Achilles' spear. This is the principle of homoeopathy. The Greek word for medicine (*pharmakon*) is virtually the same as the word for poison. Originally it meant a vegetable substance with magical powers — the magical powers that Chiron has knowledge of.

This homoeopathic principle, that the disease is cured by the substance that caused, or could cause it, is also relevant in psychotherapy. It is generally by confronting the experience that has wounded us, by really experiencing the pain of it, that we are able to integrate it and become whole again. And of course the psychotherapist, like the doctor with his knowledge of poisons or the surgeon with his knife (medical professionals are known to collaborate with torturers in many parts of the world), can use her special knowledge to inflict wounds, to put people down, find their weak spots, cause pain without healing intent. So the tools of the healer can both kill and cure.

The last main feature of Chiron is that he himself has a wound which will not heal. He has been accidentally shot by Herakles, and Herakles' arrows are dipped in the blood of the poisonous Hydra, a beast of the watery depths. Chiron is wounded in the knee or foot, and he hobbles about in perpetual pain. So here is the irony: the physician who cannot heal himself. Again this is a very important attribute of the healer. Few people get involved with healing work without having experienced a need for healing themselves and, in any case, in the process of becoming a doctor or therapist one inevitably starts to get in touch with one's own pain or sickness, one has all the symptoms in the medical dictionary, and one is likely to find some very real imperfections which won't altogether go away. And, to the extent that one remains aware of one's own sickness, one is a better healer, able to empathise with the patient and to avoid the pitfall of arrogance that immediately alienates the healer from both patient and healing process – a process the doctor facilitates rather than brings about.

So much for the myth, which I felt deserved laying out in some detail. It is probable that by this time many readers will already have made a connection between the discovery of this healer in the heavens and certain contemporary developments in the realm of health and medicine. The discovery of Chiron came at a time when in the West there was quite a health boom, with health food shops opening in the high street and a great epidemic of alternative therapies and forms of preventative medicine. New therapies of various kinds were developing apace, and many old techniques were being rediscovered or imported.

This trend came as a reaction against what had become the "orthodox" form of medicine: symptom-centred, often mechanistic and alienating, and with a tendency to split mind and body into areas of ever-increasing specialisation and a frightening subservience to the business interests of a vast and powerful pharmaceutical industry. Medicine itself had been found to be sick in many respects, leading inevitably to a search for new approaches. It was a time of crisis and change in the arts of healing.

There may well be other features of the age that relate to Chiron. I myself wonder if he has to do with such issues as ecology (healing the earth) and the animal welfare movement, for the mythological figure seems to be quite an earthy character.

At any rate, the naming of this object in the sky after the mythological wounded healer immediately interested me, and I began to put him in on my charts. (The glyph resembles a key, and this in itself has been seen as significant: Chiron as an opener of doors.) What first caught my attention was that he often seemed particularly prominent on the charts of healers and therapists, and was particularly often near the ascendant or midheaven . I therefore began to collect charts of people in these professions, and to date have compared 115 charts of healers/therapists with a similar number of non-healers. What has emerged from this is that, according to my sample, there is a great preference among health professionals (though there are not very many orthodox doctors in my sample) for certain house positions of Chiron. Statistically, one would expect that roughly the same number of charts would have Chiron in each house. In fact, the odds are very high against the deviation which the sample showed from the expected distribution. I cannot say whether my findings will be replicated by others, and am not even absolutely sure that such statistical methods are valid tools with which to analyse astrological material, but the results are certainly very interesting.

The house most often occupied by Chiron on these charts is the tenth, followed by the first, twelfth, sixth and eighth. The tenth house, of course, is traditionally associated with the vocation, and the majority of my sample were therapists by profession. Anything in the first house represents a very personal issue, right there in our environment, something we are always consciously or unconsciously grappling with, and often manifested in the body in some way, as illustrated by an example that follows shortly. The twelfth house has a mediumistic quality, planets placed there representing energies for which we are channels, but over which we have little direct control. I found that quite a lot of those with a twelfth house Chiron were healers, channels for healing energy, while most of the rest, and many of those with Chiron in the eighth, worked with the unconscious and dreams and images. The sixth house, corresponding to the sign of Virgo, is traditionally associated with health issues.

Another thing I have noticed again and again is that at turning points connected with healing, for example, a healing crisis, a breakthrough in therapy, a decision to train as a therapist or the start of some kind of therapy, there are most often progressions or transits to Chiron in operation, as if the inner healer is being awoken at such times. New therapy clients most often come to me when there are aspects to my Chiron, that is, when the healer in me is being called upon, and several times I have found the degree of my Chiron rising when I have set up a chart for the start of therapy, or sometimes Chiron is prominent on that chart, for example, exactly conjunct the midheaven. The degree of my natal Chiron was also rising when I had a curious psychic experience connected with healing. Very strong contacts involving Chiron between charts of therapists and clients are also something I run into a great deal; if Chiron in the chart in some sense represents our "inner healer", it is obviously desirable that the person we go to for help with our health is able to contact this.

I found a dramatic illustration of the theme of the wounded healer in a woman with Chiron conjunct the ascendant. Another astrologer[18] had told me that he had noticed Chiron featuring very strongly on the charts of people with physical disabilities. This lady had been damaged at birth, had little use of her legs and had later gone blind. At a point in her life when there were important progressions and transits to her Chiron she decided to train as a counsellor, as a result of hearing a programme on the radio, and pressed on with her intention in the face of enormous difficulties. As so often, it was partly her own wounds that drew her into wanting to heal others.

Chiron also features strongly on the charts of therapeutic establishments of various kinds, and having noticed that a Uranus transit over the Chiron position on the United Kingdom chart (0.00 hrs., 1 Janaury 1801, London: coming into force of the Act for the Union of Great Britain and Ireland) coincided with strikes in the National Health Service, I decided to check out what was happening at the time of the foundation of the NHS. To my astonishment I found that there were major progressed aspects to the UK Chiron from the ascendant, midheaven, sun and Venus, the ascendant-ruler.

So I feel that the connection between Chiron and therapy, in the broadest sense, is established, and I am not the only person to have been struck by this. Perhaps in a more generalised sense Chiron has to do with a very practical urge to make whole and put right what is spoiled or damaged. Then the theme of wounding must come into the picture; every planet, however "benefic", has a dark side too, and I have even found hints that Chiron may have quite a destructive side. There is also a final act to the myth which I have not yet touched on.

The end of the story concerns Prometheus, who had been punished by Zeus for stealing fire from Olympus by being tied to a rock in Tartarus, the punishment division of the underworld, and each day having an eagle peck at his liver. Chiron, being an immortal son of Kronos, yet with an incurable wound, gives his immortality to Prometheus, whereupon Prometheus is raised to the status of an Olympian god and Chiron, becoming mortal, dies. There are different possible interpretations of this act; it can be seen as a noble self-sacrifice or a world-weary gesture of defeat. At any rate, it seems to me to emphasise once again that the fate of the healer is a life close to death and suffering: doctors are among the most likely individuals to commit suicide.

With these threads of meaning, healing, hurting, wounding and death, how are we to fit Chiron into the astrological system? Can he, like the other trans-Saturnians, be awarded co-rulership of a sign? Claims have been made for a connection with Virgo (which is associated with healing), Sagittarius (whose image is a centaur), Scorpio (because of the death connection) and Libra, and probably other signs as well. It has also been suggested that this maverick body does not rule any sign.

A new planet is not to be taken aboard lightly. Exciting though I find Chiron, I am left with some misgivings, for each new planet complicates the chart and increases considerably the number of possible aspects. Perhaps we could still do with secondary rulers for Virgo and for one of the Venusian signs, but how many planets can we cope with? Some astrologers use a number of asteroids whose motion has been plotted, and it seems likely that other bodies will be found orbiting the sun; some astrologers additionally use hypothetical planets which are unknown to astronomy.

Since the discovery of Uranus we have been faced with the possibility of an ever-changing system, and some would say that astrology has been shaken off course. I would say that astrology is changing because the world is changing as never before; we cannot go back to the days before nuclear power was discovered, nor can we ignore Pluto's role on the birth chart. If astrology seems to be getting out of control with all this novelty, it is but a reflection of the times we live in.

Chapter 8

Fate and Free Will

When astrology is mentioned, nothing excites more interest or raises more anxiety than the question of whether it is possible to predict future events and, if so, whether this involves a belief that our lives are altogether fated, that is, literally decreed in advance. There is no doubt that this is a deeply disturbing thought, for if everything is predetermined and choice an illusion, what is the point of all our struggles?

You may already have noticed the paradox inherent in my propensity to read into the chart, which could have been drawn up before the child had anything much by way of a relationship with the parents, tendencies attributed to parental influence and upbringing. Traditional astrology certainly speaks of the mother and father, but does not imply that our early relationship with parents determines the characteristics we develop, although the latter are also described by the chart. This connection is rather the insight of developmental psychology. Natal astrology itself does not attribute causes, but implies that we come into this life with a pattern to live out, we arrive all set up for certain kinds of experience. In early life we will no doubt experience them through our parents, later independently. A psychology which insisted that children were born as blank sheets waiting to be written on, that nurture is all and nature nothing, would not fit easily with astrology. The horoscope presents itself as something which is given.

Fate is a feminine deity belonging to an early stratum of

mythological development. The plural form, the three Fates, is frequently found. Their Roman name was the Parcae, meaning the ones who bring forth children, indicating that they play their role in the mystery of birth, which immediately puts us in mind of the birth chart.

We find the Fates in numerous traditions, and usually they come in threes or in multiples of three. In the story of Sleeping Beauty they appear, typically, in the guise of the twelve wise women who come to the baby's birth feast and endow her with beauty, virtue, wealth and other gifts. Actually there is a double play on numbers in this story, for although the king invites twelve wise women (four times three), there is a thirteenth whom he neglects to invite, and she in her anger is the cause of the mischief that befalls Sleeping Beauty. Twelve is, of course, the number of signs of the zodiac, the number of months in the solar year, while thirteen is more nearly the number of true lunar months in the year, so that this irregular number has long been associated with lunar traditions, with witchcraft and the feminine.

Both the number thirteen and the number three, then, are associated with the moon, and with the Great Goddess who is often three-in-one, corresponding to the new, the full, and the dark face of the moon, beginning, fulness and end.

In Greek, Fate is known as Moira, meaning share or portion, or as the three Moirai. In modern Greek the related verb still means to divide, share or distribute, and also to deal cards, so your Fate is, in a sense, the hand you have been dealt.

In the three-fold version of this powerful mistress Fate, which is probably the older one, the three Moirai are associated with spinning, a task traditionally always reserved for women, and the theme of the three spinning women is another motif found in fairy tales. The three are known in Greek as Clotho, the Spinner, Lachesis, the

Apportioner, and Atropos, the Inflexible One. The first spins the thread of the individual life, the second measures it and the third cuts it off.

The image of spinning is often associated with the Goddess. She is Mother, and what she spins is Matter, two words from the same root, and so spinning is the process by which Mother Nature is imagined continuously to bring forth new substance and new life. But the moon constantly rings the changes, from new to full to darkening, and everything which is born is fated to change and eventually to die. The threefold Goddess represents change and transience, and Fate in this sense is the truth that birth (and the birth chart) marks the beginning of a process which inevitably has its end. Fate has to do with time.

Even in the classical period of Greek mythology Moira, a dark figure in the background, was seen as beyond the power of the Olympian gods and goddesses; even Zeus himself could not interfere with her dictates. The gods were not thought of as eternal; they too had their allotted share.

The question often asked is "Do you believe in fate?", but it seems to me as valid, if not more so, to ask "To what extent can we believe in free will?" "Will" originally means nothing more than wish or intention. Is free will merely wishful thinking, an illusion of choice or power? Our genetic structure predetermines our potential height and weight, our colouring, perhaps some of our psychological tendencies. The parents to whom we are born not only supply their genes and contribute to the timing of our birth but also determine much of the all-important environment of our early lives. Whether they live in the country or in town, whether they are radicals or conservatives, the nature of their relationship, their anxieties, griefs, quarrels, ambitions, will all leave their profound imprint on us.

The collective situation we are born into will also affect us, both through our parents and directly: we will develop differently according to whether it is a time of peace or of war, of prosperity or hardship, of stability or change. Our birth may be easy or difficult, we may be born with brain damage, or inherited disease, or drug-induced deformities. In none of these things do we have any choice; we are formed by forces beyond our control. We grow and age and die without having any say in the matter at all; fate in that sense, the fate of humanity, has to do with the fact that we exist in time, but so many of the individual variables also appear fated. Whether we interpret our plight as the will of God, or the outcome of original sin, or as *karma*, the result of our actions in previous lives, makes little difference to the reality of the experience, although such a framework may provide a meaningful view of the individual life as part of a greater pattern. This includes the possibility of some other kind of life where change and death do not apply.

We know that even in the age of the Goddess, when the inevitable biological round dominated the human psyche, sacrifices were made, for example the annual or biannual sacrifice of the king. Such offerings can only be seen as an attempt to placate the all-powerful one, to win her favour in the struggle for survival. Later there were to be a host of deities whose favour must be sought in the varying circumstances of life. It was felt, then, that although there was ultimately no escape from the fate of mortality there was some possibility of negotiation, some room for manoeuvre, first probably to secure a better deal for the tribe as a whole, eventually even for the individual. Such favours may still be sought today through prayer. Once Clotho has spun the thread and birth has taken place, the cut of inflexible Atropos is inevitable, but in between, in the realm of Lachesis, in the course of our lives, perhaps we are not powerless. As mentioned in Chapter 4, there are reasons to suppose that we have more power to change things now than ever before.

Much depends on our attitude. If we see ourselves as passive chess pieces in someone else's game, we are obviously going to be able to change nothing. If, on the other hand, we dare to suppose that we ourselves can make moves, always granted that we can only move according to certain rules, and cannot undo those moves already made, we permit ourselves the possibility of modifying our fate. We cannot, by sheer will-power, grow another leg if we have lost one, but we can live our one-legged life creatively, and minimise the limiting power of our affliction. Perhaps we can even come to appreciate the value and purpose of such a limitation. Just when to go along with things as they present themselves (which we might call the lunar approach), and when to try to change them and creatively participate in our own destiny (the solar approach), is partly a question of individual make-up and partly a question of timing.

The issue of fate in the context of astrology has been wrestled with since the early days of natal horoscopy. Alongside the identification of astrology with the heathen kingdom of Babylon, the question of fate has been the principal cause of hostility towards astrology from elements within the Christian Church. For the dead hand of fate the Church had substituted the more benign concept of Divine Providence, and fatalism had become a term of abuse. It was also argued that since God is good and capable only of creating good things, and since all evil comes from the exercise of human free will, under the influence of the Devil, God, in making the heavens, could not possibly have created malefic influences or signs. As God could not have predestined us to suffer, astrology, to the extent that it declares suffering to be predetermined, must be the Devil's work. So the fate versus free will debate involves a confrontation with the nature of evil and of suffering.

While I do not feel able to take up the theological debate on the nature of evil in Christian teaching, I do feel that it is important to stress once more the distinction between the word *evil*, which implies moral judgement, and the word *suffering*, which does not. That suffering is an inevitable part of the human condition, at least since the Fall, we might say part of the fate of incarnation into a mortal body, is certainly reflected in astrology, and in the Christian passion story is the mechanism for our deliverance from evil.

The birth chart can tell us something about when and where we are likely to experience difficulty and conflict, though it cannot measure the degree of our suffering. It can also help us to see meaning in our pain and thus alleviate it, and through understanding cope better with, or even resolve, some of our conflicts. What it cannot do, although there are, alas, some astrologers who would disagree with this, is enable us to make moral judgements about individuals. In other words, although astrology may speak of the weaknesses and inner stresses we are subject to, some of which might contribute to behaviour we would classify as immoral, it in no sense identifies us as inherently good or bad people. The greatest gifts can be abused and the greatest hardships can inspire positive attitudes and actions. Each planet, sign, house or aspect is morally neutral and each has a positive and negative mode of expression.

Although astrology can be and has been used to deny individual responsibility for actions, this reflects a particular attitude in those practising the art and is in no way inherent in astrology itself. In this respect as in many others, astrology reflects back to us the attitude with which we approach it.

The Stoic philosophers, to whom we largely owe the continuation of the astrological tradition at an important stage in the development of natal astrology, certainly believed in fate, but also in the possibility of moral excellence through the uncomplaining acceptance of it. The meaning of the word "stoic", as we use it today, implies an attitude of noble resignation to what cannot be changed. However, we do not need to accept with the Stoics the view that the predictability of planetary *movements* necessitates a belief in the total predictability of *events*.

Fate, as we have seen, has to do with time, the realm in particular of Saturn and of the moon. The timing of transits and progressions is certainly predictable. This year I have to confront Pluto, next year I will encounter Uranus. No effort will persuade my Pluto transit to call some other time, or bring forward a progression of the sun to Venus by five years.

Yet timing is one thing and symbolism another. The first can be measured precisely, the second cannot. The coming together of certain planetary symbols does not describe a particular concrete event. Rather it tells us something about the nature of the time and of the opportunities and lessons open to us at that stage. A likelihood of events of a certain nature is implied, but such "events" fit into the unfolding of our own nature, and how we experience and relate to a particular transit or progression will depend to a considerable degree on our level of self-understanding and the way we have lived our life to date. It sometimes seems to me that an event such as a serious illness or accident is a last desperate attempt on the part of the psyche to force us to confront issues we have been avoiding. I would not pretend that all such misfortunes can be avoided, but many can if we listen to our inner warnings. The advance notice astrology affords can similarly be heeded, so that we are ready to move with the current rather than against it. The degree to which we can influence events, however, remains an unknown quantity, and although we may be able to negotiate with fate, it should not be supposed that we can outsmart it. Many people armed with a good understanding of astrology have planned moves aimed at manipulating transits in a desired direction, only in the end to be surprised, even thwarted. This is not necessarily a bad thing, for what we would have chosen for ourselves in our limited understanding may not always be what is best for us.

I have also noticed that transits and progressions tend to manifest more often on a purely inner level in the case of older people, particularly those with some degree of self-awareness. Younger people with less life experience are more inclined to act out their transits, or to experience them as events which happen to them inexplicably. But events do not just happen; they happen to *people*, and the events that happen to us often speak volumes about us, and about what aspects of ourselves are crying out to be dealt with. It is certainly pertinent to ask, "Why me?", but with an openness to finding an answer and a willingness to see a purpose to our experiences. The person who, for example, is always getting things stolen may be inviting exploitation because he feels undeserving.

An event, the inner process it is connected to, and the astrological symbolism of the time all reflect each other. But, from the point of view of the individual to whom the event happens, the inner experience is ultimately the most important.

I would not deny that future events are sometimes predicted using astrology and other means, but in my experience even the most gifted psychics are wrong a good proportion of the time. This suggests to me that their predictions are based more on probability than on certainty, and that we generally have some room to manoeuvre. In fact, perhaps probability, an important concept in modern physics, offers us a way out of the fate/free will dichotomy. We could say that astrology expresses the probability of events of a certain kind, and that we, as conscious individuals, can influence the odds as a skilful card player can influence the outcome of a poker game.

I once worked with a man on the interpretation of a dream he had had. The background to the dream was that his mother, who had considerable psychic ability and had always proved accurate in predicting deaths, had recently informed him that she had always known he would die before she did, and she was now an old woman. Though shaken, the son felt he still had much to do in this life and was determined to challenge this predicted fate. Difficult times did in fact lie just ahead of him, but he met them with a willingness to adapt. In the dream he attended his mother's funeral, suggesting that the decision to outlive her and not to be bound by her prediction had the backing of his unconscious resources, that it was deeply rooted in him. Subsequently his mother told him that she had now decided that she had for once been mistaken, and that he would after all outlive her, and he felt very strongly that his own response to the prediction had been a factor in defeating it. The ensuing crisis he had to deal with was a kind of symbolic death, but he re-emerged into a new way of life. I do not know the astrological factors involved, but it sounds very much as though this period in his life corresponded to a Pluto transit.

There are astrologers who seek to avoid fatalism in natal astrology by emphasising the importance of the moment of interpretation and the interaction between astrologer and horoscope, diminishing the substantiality of the chart and denying its function as a strict time map based on cyclic processes. This school sees *horary* or oracular astrology as the primary form of the art and views a reading of the birth chart as an extension of horary practice. The chart is not seen as being fundamentally connected to the individual born at the corresponding time, but is read, rather as one might read tea-leaves, as being relevant at the moment of reading.

This approach has a certain appeal, but it does not entirely avoid the issue of fate in the sense of "what has been decreed", for horary is regularly used to answer questions about future events; the practice, in fact, lends itself much more than natal astrology to precise prediction. It is only a matter of degree between the notion of something being decreed at the time of an individual's birth or at or before the time of asking a horary question. In any case, as has already been remarked, we *are* born with certain characteristics and limitations, so there is a very real element of predetermination in our lives. Beyond this there is considerable flexibility and room for choice, and this is not denied by astrological symbolism, even when timing is seen as predetermined.

If the symbolism of fate connects with the symbolism of the moon and Saturn, will-power is generally associated with the sun and Mars, while freedom is traditionally the realm of Jupiter. As this is an ancient dichotomy I am leaving aside the trans-Saturnian planets, although they may also be fitted into such a schema![9] Suffice it to say that the clash between the two tendencies is inherent in the astrological language itself, and can be experienced within each of us.

Time, the domain of Saturn and reflected in the strict, inflexible progress of the planets, connects us to fate, but symbolism belongs to Jupiter, who sees not only meaning but also infinite possibilities. It seems to me that we are caught between the two, each exerting its pull on us. If we overuse our Jupiterian freedom we will eventually come crashing down to Saturnian reality, but in the acceptance of our limitations there is a kind of freedom too.

Chapter 9

The Wider Context

Natal astrology is far and away the most popular form of the art, reflecting a considerable interest in the nature and destiny of the individual. Nothing conveys better than the birth horoscope the necessary uniqueness and unrepeatability of each new being, and it offers at the same time a framework for understanding and valuing individual differences.

Astrologer and Client

The value of natal astrology depends to a considerable extent on the approach of the individual astrologer, for she or he is also unique and will have a particular astrological background. Astrology is not one but many, with numerous schools, sometimes hostile to each other, and one would be hard-pressed to define a central area of common agreement.

The approach outlined in this book is that of an individual who is interested in people rather than events, and who views people as essentially psychological beings, with a capacity to influence as well as be influenced by circumstances. An astrologer working in a more traditional framework might reject many of my assumptions. A Hindu astrologer, coming from a more fatalistic society, once assured me that astrology had nothing whatever to do with psychology but was simply the "science of events". Both of us are dealing with the same "reality", human life and experience, but we have very different constructs of the nature of that reality.

Quite apart from her conscious and unconscious assumptions about the nature of astrology and of the world we live in, the astrologer brings to the reading of a birth chart all her own prejudices and shortcomings. Just as the uninformed latch onto a sun-sign classification to pigeonhole people and perpetuate stereotypes, so more sophisticated astrologers can often be heard to condemn an individual on account of a Venus in Scorpio or a moon/Saturn square, rather than being open to the configuration's potential for positive expression. Similarly, astrology is often used by people to justify their own failings ("I can't help being bossy, I've got Leo rising").

The astrologer is the imperfect interpreter through whom astrology must speak. The better the astrologer appreciates the peculiar quality of her own way of seeing things the less likely she is to impose her own prejudices on those whose charts she interprets, and the better she can facilitate the process of discovery in those whose charts she reads. Such self-knowledge can come through astrology itself. Each birth chart should be a reminder of the fact that we cannot all be measured by the same yardstick, but serve different purposes and hold different values, and our own chart can constantly reveal more about ourselves. Personal psychotherapy, however, can also be a useful tool of self-knowledge for the astrologer, and has the advantage of leaving less room for self-deception. It is extraordinary how blind we can be to our own prejudices, even when they are staring up at us from our birth chart. The experience of psychotherapy is also a good foil for the inflation astrology tends to promote in the practitioner.

The client also comes to a reading with all kinds of hidden assumptions. Primary among these is usually the belief in the mysterious power of the astrologer, a belief very often in the astrologer's total omniscience. It is rather like the passive expectation of a patient in a doctor's surgery that the professional has all the answers and can prescribe easily swallowed remedies for all ills. The unwary astrologer can easily be seduced by the power of the situation into making dogmatic pronouncements and proffering high-handed advice.

There seems to be a law according to which an astrologer with problems she has not worked out for herself will inevitably attract clients with similar problems, and it is just when the astrologer finds herself urgently impressing upon a client the need for a particular attitude or course of action that she needs to ask herself whether the advice is not really more appropriate for herself than for the individual whose chart she is reading.

It is, in fact, a debatable issue whether it is the astrologer's job to offer advice at all. To use a chart-reading as an advice-giving session is to encourage the client to feel dependent on outside help rather than enabling him to make his own decisions based on an appreciation of the options open to him.

Perhaps the most useful thing an astrologer can do for a client is to connect him with the symbolism of the horoscope, and through it with the symbolic dimension in his own life. Despite the complexity of a chart, the individual images that arise from it have great power and depth and can speak to the untrained as well as to the trained, particularly when they are related to life experience and events.

It is in the dialogue between astrologer and client that the chart really comes to life. For this reason a written reading sent by post to an unknown client is a poor second best, though it may still be valuable and surprisingly accurate. Probably the least helpful kind of reading is an "identikit" computer printout. This may be useful to the student of astrology exploring the details of his own chart, and provide a basis for asking further questions, but a computer program lacks the human ability to synthesise and prioretise symbolic information intuitively.

Variety of Techniques

Different approaches to astrological practice lead to and combine with a great variety of different techniques, from which every astrologer has to select. There are ten or more systems in common use for determining house cusps; there is more than one zodiac; there is disagreement about the number of planets worthy of consideration and, in the case of newer planets, about their nature too; the number and meaning of types of aspect and the degree of precision required in defining them are also disputed. On top of these considerations there is a wide repertoire of additional factors used by different astrologers, such as minor divisions of the zodiac, and the so-called Arabian parts which are derived from combinations of planetary positions. Modern astrology has introduced new interpretive elements such as midpoints, also calculated from the positions of the planets, and more recently harmonics.

The concept of harmonics[20] in astrology was developed by a leading British astrologer of this century, John Addey, who had a vision of an astrology which would not only break down the divisions between different schools but would reconcile astrology with science. He redefined the basic elements of astrology using the principles of wave theory and developed what might be termed a neo-Pythagorean system in which the meaning of number became all-important. Aspects in particular were reframed as proportions of the circle productive of a particular resonance, much as musical intervals are defined as mathematical divisions of the octave. Using this system a series of secondary charts can be produced from the original natal chart, to provide deeper and more detailed information.

Beyond the Birth Chart

Our own birth chart is the place where most of us start with astrology, and rightly so, but we are also parts of something greater than ourselves: we live in the context of society and of the world at large. It is an essential feature of the rich symbolic language of astrology that it can be a bridge between different levels of experience and between subjects that are otherwise difficult to relate to each other. The planetary principles can be seen at work not only in the human psyche but in the natural world, in the course of history, in the realm of ideas or wherever we look with the imaginal eye. There is a Mars dimension to life, a quality of heat and fiery energy, of sharpness, thrust and force, which can express itself in chilli sauce, a stinging criticism, a war, a conflagration, or an upsurge of passion. Viewed from the perspective of natal or birth chart astrology the symbolism we perceive in outer events, and which is reflected in the chart, may have a subjective meaning; but the individual birth chart need not be our focus.

SYNASTRY

If we start with the individual chart and begin to make connections outwards, we employ the technique of *synastry*, that is, we compare one set of astrological data with another. Most commonly, this technique is used to compare the birth charts of two individuals. Synastry of this kind is traditionally accorded a very important place in Indian society in the arrangement of marriages, and the Western astrologer, too, is often approached by couples researching the vexed question of "compatibility".

The first thing to be considered is each individual chart and what it has to say about basic tendencies and partnership needs – some of us might have severe problems in any kind of partnership. Next comes comparison of the overall pattern of the two charts and the question of compatibility or lack of it. This involves a delicate appreciation of the factors that can make or break a relationship. Some signs get on better with each other than others, but too much harmony and similarity can lead to boredom, and some people thrive on conflict.

Two people with a concentration on the same element (that is, on fiery, earthy, airy, or watery signs), while they may have numerous mutual trines on their charts, may also run into problems. Two people with a lot of earth on their charts might soon start looking elsewhere for some levity, while two without any planets in earth signs might come to grief because each was looking to the other to sort out practical issues so that the gas bill never got paid. Complementarity is as important as similarity.

The most important factor in chart comparison is the combination of the aspect patterns. Just as my sun may be square my own Neptune, so it might be trine my partner's Jupiter, and we will both experience that trine in our relationship. Each inter-aspect makes its own statement. You will probably feel uncomfortable if my Saturn conjuncts your moon, as when you are at your most natural you will feel some sort of withdrawal or disapproval coming from me. I, on the other hand, will be experiencing your way of being as somehow threatening, undermining my defences, making me conscious of what I would rather hide. It is rather like living with a permanent transit. If your Jupiter trines my sun, having you around will feel like a permanent Jupiter transit to me, opening up new possibilities for me, while I am stimulating you to seek and explore.

Of vital importance, too, is how willing we are to change and to work on the relationship, and this is not necessarily something we can find in the chart. Two people with a predominance of fixed signs, with squares and oppositions between them, could really dig their heels in and destroy each other, but it would not be impossible for them to use their determination to push each other towards greater self-awareness and learn to respect and make allowance for each other's stubbornness. It would, however, require a strong desire to make the relationship work. Similarly, the more aware we are of the needs and expectations we as individuals bring to a partnership, the better we will be at working through any difficulties.

Despite this stricture, synastry is one of the areas where research has indicated the validity of astrologically based judgement. From a thousand questionnaires filled in by married couples to determine how happy they were as partners, ten with a very high score and ten with a very low score were selected as the basis for an experiment. Ten astrologers were given the birth data of the couples and ten psychologists were given the results of personality tests on the couples, and both groups of professionals were asked to discern which were the happy and which the unhappy couples. While both psychologists and astrologers scored higher than chance, the astrologers were the more accurate[21].

Synastry is not only of value in marriage-type relationships, but can offer insight into problems between different members of a family, suggest how a child can best be supported by the parents, or which of their sore spots it is likely to hit, and what its contribution to the family system may be. One social worker I know successfully uses astrology to help in matching child and parents for adoption. In the case of blood parents, the child's birth chart represents transits to the parents' charts at the time of the child's birth, so that the aspects formed by the child's chart to that of a parent can be seen as transits whose effects can go on for a very long time. Synastry can also be an aid in recruiting members of a team, or in weighing up a prospective business partnership.

GROUPS AND ENTERPRISES

An individual birth chart can also be compared with a chart which is not the birth horoscope of a person, but, for example, the birth chart of an enterprise or of a group of some kind: a political party, a club, or a business organisation. The birth chart of such a collective can be used as an aid in understanding the inherent strengths and weaknesses of the group, as well as to predict likely developments on the basis of progressions and transits. One obvious difference between the chart of an individual and that of a group is that an individual, through self-awareness and conscious effort, has a greater degree of freedom to steer a course, while groups, especially large ones, are far less wieldy. It is a wise decision, when some new collective enterprise is being set up, to use the astrological art of *election* to choose a propitious starting point. Here the task is to select the most auspicious chart. This practice has been carried out in founding nations and cities, but it can also be used for enterprises of a personal nature. In such cases, synastry between the birth chart and the proposed electional chart, in other words the transits the latter represents to the former, should also be considered.

MUNDANE ASTROLOGY

Continuing to widen our frame of reference, we come to political or *mundane* astrology. The earliest astrology we know of was concerned with matters of state, and it is still generally accepted that individual fates can be overpowered by collective forces: we would not expect a world war, for example, to show up on every individual chart. This means that mundane astrology is of very great importance. At the time of writing we are all of us at the mercy of decisions made by leaders of the superpowers, the United States and the Soviet Union, so that developments on their national charts indirectly affect us all.

Problems arise in determining the birth of a nation, and sometimes several national charts may need to be considered. In Britain the chart of the United Kingdom (Act of Union, 1801) is probably the most important one, but the chart of the coronation of William the Conqueror (1066) is still sometimes used. In the case of a country which gains independence from colonial rule the issue may appear to be easier, but even here one runs into difficulties. The United States Declaration of Independence was signed by the majority of signatories in the morning, but the last to append his signature did so in the afternoon, and the chart for the latter time, with Sagittarius rising, speaks much more potently of the nation than the earlier, Gemini-rising chart which has often been assumed to be the correct one.

Successive charts for new regimes governing the same people have a way of picking up on the temperament of the people, such as the Capricorn sun on the UK chart, which reflects the traditional stiff upper lip. Astrologers at least since the time of Ptolemy have allotted the astrological rulership of nations of the known world to the various signs of the zodiac, but these allocations have been modified with increased knowledge of distant parts as well as with changes of boundaries and populations. Ptolemy's system of geographical rulerships is based on a division of the known world into quarters, one of which is the domain of what we now know as the fire signs, one of the earth signs, and so forth. Within each quarter, individual territories are deemed to belong to one of the three signs in the triplicity, or element group. Britain, for example, falls in the fiery quarter and comes under the sign of Aries.

In early Mesopotamian astrology, as we have seen, the welfare of the nation was vested in the king. In addition to charts for nations, charts of leaders are also part of the stock-in-trade of mundane astrology. It has been said, perhaps harshly, that a nation gets the government it deserves and, particularly where the leadership depends on a popular vote, the people must be held responsible for the kind of leadership they get. A particular leader comes to the fore in response to the popular mood, and it is interesting, sometimes chastening, to consider what semi-conscious purpose we are acting out in electing a particular individual to the highest office. A nation or other collective has its own psychological life, an inner history that runs in parallel to and influences the outer one. In times of confusion and feelings of helplessness a strong leader is sought, in times of humiliation a heroic leader, in times of depression a leader who knows how to raise morale. When the nation feels confident it can afford to be more liberal. Much may be gleaned about the tendencies of the time from the progressions and transits to the national chart. Another dimension is that national leaders, particularly those who make a strong impact, tend to have strong synastric connections between their own charts and the chart of the country they represent.

HORARY ASTROLOGY

Up to here we have been principally concerned with charts which represent the birth of something, a person, a nation, a business, but astrology has an application in which the notion of birth is not necessarily involved. Horary astrology is used to answer questions, and the chart is drawn up for the time and place at which the question is asked. One could define this as the birth of the question, but this is a somewhat clumsy notion. To say that the question's moment has arrived is perhaps to express it better.

Not every horary chart can be satisfactorily interpreted, perhaps because we are not always attuned to that mysterious sense which draws us to the right moment like a dowser's stick to water, perhaps because we are asking about future events which are simply not yet knowable. In horary astrology certain features are taken to indicate that no answer is possible, that it is too early or too late to ask that particular question, or that the person who asked the question is withholding relevant and essential information. Often what appear to be chance obstructions may deflect a question until the appropriate time. To give an example, I recently gave the telephone number of a skilled horary astrologer to some friends who wanted help in making an important decision. They lost the telephone number, so had to contact me again, and could not get hold of me immediately. The time at which they posed the question to the astrologer was thus several days later than they would have chosen, but through this delay they stumbled upon the right time for the question. This issue of the "right moment" comes up in the timing of natal consultations, too. Nor are such instances of unconscious timing restricted to astrological situations, but astrology alerts us to that inner process which guides us to circumstances at the appropriate moment, according to our needs—or if you will to our deserts.

Horary depends to a far greater extent than does natal astrology, as it is commonly practised today, on the application of precise and complex traditional rules. Almost invariably, the area of interest will show up in the first glance at the chart, so that if it is a career question the tenth house is likely to be strongly tenanted, or the seventh, if it is to do with partnership. It is not, however, the first glance that counts in providing the answer to the question; the planets which are the *significators* of the important elements in the question must be determined according to the rules, and other planets may be ignored.

A skilled horary astrologer can provide quite elaborate answers, for an astrological chart contains extremely complex and detailed information, and the timing of developments can often be accurately ascertained as well as their nature. The full range of astrological symbolism can be experienced through horary, as it is applied to the most varied of subjects and situations, and all the associations of planets, signs and houses come into play, colours, substances, compass directions, plants, animals, professions, and many more. A favourite question concerns the whereabouts of a missing person or object, and I was particularly impressed when a friend expert in the field helped me to find a lost cat. From the chart she was able to deduce the colour of the cat and the fact that it had left via the kitchen door, as well as its imprisonment in a dark, damp place "not above ground level" (the lumber room in the next-door block of flats), the approximate time it would take me to find it, and the fact that some coaxing would be needed, and the help of an intermediary (a resident in the flats).

The horary chart itself connects with the complex life of the individual. The person who asks the question (the *querent*) is represented in the chart by the planet which rules the ascendant. Often, when the question is particularly pertinent, the rising degree will be one which features importantly in the querent's natal chart. The sign and house position of the ascendant ruler and its contact with other planets may make statements not only about the external features of the querent's situation in relation to a personal question, but also about his motivation.

EVENTS

Charts are also often set up for events, and many suggest aspects of the event additional to those already known, for example, causal factors in a disaster. Events interest us to the extent that they affect people, and we would expect the chart of an event that strongly affects an individual or a nation to make strong contacts to the natal chart in question. Here again we are dealing with chart comparison, or with transits. The following incident illustrates the mysterious interplay between individual and event, between inner and outer reality.

The incident concerns a woman's dream and an external event which coincided with it. In the dream she is poring over an antique map. She knows she should be protecting the "heir". The heir turns out to be an heiress, who is in danger. A big iron vehicle carrying enemies approaches, lumbering over a stretch of sand. A shot rings out. The dreamer knows the heiress is dead, and yet simultaneously that she is not *really* dead but will be all right. At the sound of the shot the dreamer awoke, aware that there had been a bang on the window. She noticed the time on the clock, and being an astrologer herself had the presence of mind to note the time so that a chart could be drawn up. Lying in the dark, her fear was that a bird had crashed into the window and must inevitably have been killed. In the morning she apprehensively drew back the curtains and saw on the sill, to her amazement, a dove – a bird which does not usually fly at night. It had survived its impact with the glass and eventually flew off, apparently undamaged. The chart for the event had Venus prominently on the ascendant, in its own sign of Libra, and conjunct Pluto. Mars was in the twelfth house.

I tried at first to listen to the dream. Interpreting it psychologically, it seems to be speaking of an aspect of the dreamer's psychic life (the heiress) which is very vulnerable. The task of protecting it seems doomed to failure, as it cannot help but be overpowered by the brutal inhabitants of the iron vehicle. Perhaps these represent some destructive component of the dreamer's psyche which has got the upper hand. The fact that they are beyond her power to control suggests that we are dealing with something she is not conscious of. Or they may refer to crushing forces she is experiencing in the external world. Iron is the metal of Mars, and Mars on the chart for this double event is in the twelfth house, one of whose traditional designations is the house of "hidden enemies", and which often relates to things beyond our control. The dream promises, though, that while the "enemy" may win in the short term, the heiress will be all right. A death and rebirth is implied. I wondered also about the words "heir" and "heiress". Together with the old map, there seems to be a suggestion of inheritance; perhaps we are dealing with some issue that runs in the family. Or again there may be a play on words. Puns are a common feature of dreams. Is it something "airy" that is endangered, something which needs air to breathe, or some "winged" aspect of herself? Here I recalled the airborne creature on the window-sill and the air sign (Libra) rising on the chart of the moment.

Then I looked at the dreamer's chart for more clues: what is striking is that there are several transits to Venus at the time of the dream, and that on the natal chart Venus is closely squared by Pluto. Perhaps some change is going on in her way of relating to people, or within a particular relationship. Dreams and myths usually present relatedness as feminine. The death and rebirth symbolism of Pluto always connects for her with that of Venus, so perhaps the clash indicated by the dream is the present version of a recurrent struggle, which is likely to erupt under transits and progressions to the Venus/Pluto square.

Given the transits to this aspect on the dreamer's chart, it is the more striking that Venus is conjunct Pluto on the event chart. The dove is traditionally ruled by Venus, and is often used to symbolise love. Both the airy nature of the bird and the issue of relationship are emphasised by the sign Libra, in which Venus and the ascendant fall. The conjunction of Venus with Pluto symbolises the close brush with death of both the dove and the dream figure.

I could devote a great many words to speculating on what the dream and the dream-like outer event might mean to the dreamer, and to exploring other astrological features of the case; I hope, though, that the above account suffices to convey the astonishing "coincidence" involved. Should we say that the outer event reflects the inner state of the dreamer, along the lines I have suggested, or should we perhaps look at it from the dove's point of view and see the dream as mirroring the drama at the window? How is it that the astrology of the moment describes both? Astrology brings us back again and again to such unanswerable questions, which tantalise the grasping mind, and yet point in a strangely satisfying way towards an order that lies beyond our understanding.

Through symbolism, and through that mysterious law which ensures that each thing has its own time, astrology links the innermost experiences of individuals with collective issues and events. In an age of fragmentation it awakens an old vision of a universe in which all things are related and have their particular part to play, and all things are variations on relatively simple themes.

NOTES

1 See Edward Edinger: *Ego and Archetype*, Putnam, 1972. The point is illustrated with actual children's drawings.

2 See Gerald S. Hawkins: *Stonehenge Decoded*, Souvenir Press, 1966.

3 See Chris Morgan: "From Sundial to Atomic Clock" in *The Book of Time*, ed. C. Wilson, Westbridge Books, 1980.

4 By Liz Greene, co-director of the Centre for Psychological Astrology in London.

5 But see for an interesting account Erich Neumann's *The Origin and History of Consciousness*, Princeton University Press, 1966.

6 Marie-Louise von Franz: *On Divination and Synchronicity*, Inner City Books, Toronto, 1980.

7 On this subject see Joseph Campbell: *Occidental Mythology*, Part I: "The Age of the Goddess", Viking Press, 1964.

8 For example, the experiments of Frank A. Brown of Northwestern University: see article in *Science*, 4 December 1959 (US). See also Gay Gaer Luce: *Body Time*, Paladin, 1973. Various articles on plant growth in relation to the moon and planets by Nick Kollerstrom and Simon Best can be found in the *Astrological Journal* and *Correlation* (UK).

9 Nick Kollerstrom: *Astrochemistry: A Study of Metal Planet Affinities*, Emergence Press, 1984.

10 Frank McGillion: *The Opening Eye*, Coventure, London, 1980.

11 Quantum theory has been developed to explain the behaviour of sub-atomic particles, which is baffling and paradoxical. For example, particles can also be understood as waves, although these are contradictory concepts; the movement of particles can only be expressed in terms of probability; quantum interactions between the observing apparatus and what is observed make it impossible to measure all aspects of the latter simultaneously; for instance, the location and speed of a particle cannot both be ascertained. For a simple account of the New Physics, see Fritjof Capra: *The Tao of Physics*, Fontana, 1976.

12 David Bohm: *Wholeness and the Implicate Order*, Routledge & Kegan Paul, 1980.

13 Greater detail on the subject can be found in *Saturn and Melancholy* by R. Klibansky, E. Panofsky & F. Saxl, Nelson, 1964.

14 Charles Carter: *Astrological Aspects*, L.N. Fowler & Co. Ltd., 1930.

15 Zipporah Dobbyns: *Finding the Person in the Horoscope*, TIA Publications, California, 1930.

16 By Liz Greene.

17 Alan Oken: *Complete Astrology*, Bantam, 1980.

18 Howard Sasportas, co-director of the Centre for Psychological Astrology, London.

19 For a study of Pluto as the planet of Fate, see Liz Greene: *The Astrology of Fate*, Unwin, 1984.

20 John Addey: *Harmonics in Astrology*, L.N. Fowler Ltd., 1976.

21 Beverley Steffert: "Marital Bliss or Misery. Can Synastry Distinguish?", *Astrological Journal*, Summer 1983.

22 An account is given by the horary astrologer in question, Olivia Barclay, in "A Natal Astrologer's Guide to Horary" in *Transit*, magazine of the Astrological Association of Great Britain, May 1985.

COURSES

The Faculty of Astrological Studies, BM Box 7470, London WC1N 3XX, offers a broad study programme, concentrating on natal astrology, with the possibility of attaining a widely recognised diploma. Courses by correspondence or in London classes.

The Centre for Psychological Astrology, 26 Estelle Road, London NW3, runs one-day seminars and a diploma course in psychological astrology. Intended for those with a basic knowledge of natal astrology, but most seminars are of value to people with little astrological training.

Qualifying Horary Correspondence Course, c/o Olivia Barclay, Mongeham Lodge Cottage, Great Mongeham, Deal, Kent. This course is intended primarily for those who already have a basic knowledge of astrology.

SOME SUGGESTED READING

General

Derek and Julia Parker: *The New Compleat Astrologer*, Mitchell Beazley, 1984.

Tad Mann: *The Round Art*, Dragon's World, 1979.

Cherry Gilchrist: *Astrology*, History in Focus series, Batsford, 1982.

Natal Astrology

Liz Greene: *Star Signs for Lovers*, Arrow Books, 1980.

Alan Oken: *Alan Oken's Complete Astrology*, Bantam, 1980.

Jeff Mayo: *Astrology*, Teach Yourself Books, Hodder and Stoughton, 1979.

Charles E.O. Carter: *Essays on the Foundations of Astrology*, Theosophical Publishing House, 1978 (1949).

Horary Astrology

William Lilly: *Christian Astrology*, Regulus, UK, 1985. (Reprint of seventeenth-century text.)

Barbara H. Watters: *Horary Astrology and the Judgment of Events*, Valhalla, 1973.

History of Astrology

Nicholas Campion: *An introduction to the History of Astrology*, Institute for the Study of Cycles in World Affairs, London, 1982.

Mundane Astrology

Michael Baigent, Nicholas Campion and Charles Harvey: *Mundane Astrology*, Aquarian, 1984.

Philosophy of Astrology

Liz Greene: *The Astrology of Fate*, Unwin, 1984.

Science and Astrology

Michel Gauquelin: *Cosmic Influences on Human Behaviour*, Futura Publications Ltd., 1974.

Nicholas Kollerstrom: *Astrochemistry: A Study of Metal Planet Affinities*, Emergence Press, 1984.

GLOSSARY

Angles: The four points (ascendant, descendant, midheaven and I.C.) which form a cross on the chart. Their location in the zodiac depends on the earth's rotation and hence on the precise place and time of day for which the chart is drawn up.

Ascendant: The sign and degree of the zodiac rising over the horizon. The rising sign is considered an important factor in interpretation. The ascendant is one of the angles of the chart and the cusp of the first house.

Aspects: Significant angular relationships between two or more planets, e.g. conjunction, opposition.

Conjunction: An aspect. Two planets are said to be in conjunction when they are within a few degrees of each other in the zodiac. Usually they are in the same sign. The relative verb is to conjoin or conjunct.

Cusp: The boundary between one house (or sign) and the next. The second house cusp is the one lying between the first and second houses, and so forth.

Degrees: Since a circle consists of 360 degrees, there are 30 degrees in each sign of the zodiac.

Elements, Four (also known as **triplicities**): Three signs of the zodiac are assigned to each of the four elements, fire, earth, air and water. In earlier times the planets were allotted to the elements.

Horary astrology: The oracular use of astrology, which involves casting a chart for the moment a question is asked, in order to read from it the answer to the question.

Midheaven or M.C. (Medium Coeli): The culminating sign and degree of the zodiac, due south in the northern hemisphere and shown near the top of the chart. One of the four angles of the chart and in most systems the cusp of the tenth house.

Mundane astrology: Political astrology, which involves the use, among others, of national charts and charts of political leaders.

Natal astrology: The branch of astrology concerned with birth charts of individuals.

Native: The individual whose birth chart (or nativity) is under consideration.

Node: A point of intersection. The north and south nodes of the moon, otherwise known as the Dragon's Head and Dragon's Tail, are used in interpretation, though they are understood in different ways by different astrologers. They are the points where the apparent paths of the sun and moon intersect. The sun and moon have to be on these points at full or new moon for an eclipse to take place.

Opposition: An aspect, considered difficult. Two planets are in opposition when they are approximately 180 degrees apart and usually in opposite signs of the zodiac. The verb is "to oppose".

Planetary Dignities: Each planet rules one or more signs and is also said to be exalted, i.e. particularly well placed, in one sign. In the signs opposite to these it is said to be badly placed, in its detriment and fall, respectively:

Planet	Rulership	Exaltation	Detriment	Fall
Sun	Leo	Aries	Aquarius	Libra
Moon	Cancer	Taurus	Capricorn	Scorpio
Mercury	Gemini, Virgo	Virgo	Sagittarius, Pisces	Pisces
Venus	Taurus, Libra	Pisces	Scorpio, Aries	Virgo
Mars	Aries, Scorpio	Capricorn	Libra, Taurus	Cancer
Jupiter	Sagittarius, Pisces	Cancer	Gemini, Virgo	Capricorn
Saturn	Capricorn, Aquarius	Libra	Cancer, Leo	Aries
Uranus	Aquarius		Leo	
Neptune	Pisces		Virgo	
Pluto	Scorpio		Taurus	

Planets: Traditionally there were seven planets, including the sun and moon, but modern astrology incorporates the extra-Saturnians, Uranus, Neptune and Pluto, and sometimes additional bodies such as asteroids.

Progression: A method by which planets are slowly advanced to new positions for each year of life and used as a basis for forecasting developments.

Qualities (also known as **quadruplicities**): Four signs of the zodiac belong to each of the three qualities, cardinal, fixed and mutable.

Retrograde: Due to the relative movements of the earth and planets, all except the sun and moon appear from time to time to go retrograde or backwards along the zodiac.

Sign: One of the twelve divisions of the zodiac.

Square: An aspect of approximately 90 degrees, considered difficult and usually connecting signs of the same quality. The verb "to square" is also used.

Sun sign: The sign in which the sun is placed at birth, which is known from the month of birth. Sun-sign astrology is the form popular in newspapers and magazines, based on this single factor.

Synastry: The comparison of two charts to explore the relationship between them.

Transits: The positions of planets in the sky at a given time relative to the natal chart, used in forecasting.

Trine: An aspect of approximately 120 degrees, considered helpful, and usually linking planets in the same element. The corresponding verb is "to trine".

Zodiac: A circular band of the sky straddling the apparent path of the sun around the earth, along which the planets move and which is divided into 12 sections of 30 degrees known as the signs.

INDEX